RAISING SIX AND SOMEWHAT SANE

To my Friend, Barbara,

Love Barbara

RAISING SIX AND SOMEWHAT SANE

BARBARA AQUILA

authorHOUSE®

AuthorHouse™
1663 Liberty Drive
Bloomington, IN 47403
www.authorhouse.com
Phone: 1-800-839-8640

Published by AuthorHouse   02/24/2012

ISBN: 978-1-4685-5818-0 (sc)
ISBN: 978-1-4685-5817-3 (e)

CHAPTER ONE

YOU THINK YOU KNOW
YOUR MOTHER, BUT . . .

It's true what they say, that you don't realize what you've got until it's gone. Whoever said that is truly wise and must have had a lot of regrets. Funny thing about regrets, the only way you can be free of them is to let them fly away into the abyss of forgetting. We hold onto them even though they hurt us again and again as if the incident happened just yesterday instead of three months, three years, three decades ago. If we could only just let go. Regrets are like cancer; they eat you alive, gobble up all your good thoughts and roadblock your path to peace. See, we have to learn to take detours and then get right back on the road to peace of mind. This is my story, one filled with many roadblocks and it took years to discover I had a detour to travel, and that getting to where you are supposed to be cannot be dictated by years or situations, or other people's opinions of who you are, even if other people is your own family. Each of us has a life's journey that is unique and truly our own It is unfair to compare it with anyone else's. To do so is cruel because naturally you will put yourself down. I have discovered that we must love ourselves first before we can love another. In loving ourselves, we learn to be kind and merciful and forgiving. It starts with us. No, I am not like So and So; I am me, and there is no other who is exactly like me, just like no two snowflakes are the same. My mistakes are mine, as are my failures, as are my successes. Don't ever let other people define who you are, and don't ever believe that you are your career and the sum of your salary. That's not who you are; that's only what you have for awhile. Life here is temporal; when we pass on, we cannot bring our credentials or our money with us. It doesn't matter for all eternity. What we keep is who we are, our character, our heart, our mind; in other words, our spirit. We are spirits who have a body, first an earthly one, then an eternal one. Never forget this. What happens to us on earth is not as important as our reaction to it. Life is all about how much we love and that includes loving ourselves. We are made in God's image! What's not to love!

So this is my story, a shy girl with zero confidence who was destined to meet her soul mate and bare six children who looked up to her for everything they needed. I had to rise to the moment, each moment of every day until my children were grown. And then some. To understand what a monumental feat this was for me and for every parent, we need to go back to the beginning . . .

It had been told to me that my mother, Anna, took one last cup of very black coffee before the great pain gripped her that sent my father, Tony, into a whirlwind to get my mom to Bon Secour Hospital on time. The thought of Mom giving birth in his red and white 1950 Ford Sedan did not thrill him. From the time it took Tony to press the button on the elevator and then exit onto the floor, I was born, on September 8, 1951, in Baltimore Maryland, the year Harry Truman was still president. Tony, a World War Two Navy Veteran and Anna, retired from The Telephone Company to raise a family, had their first baby girl. Johnny was three years old and was probably hoping for a baby brother. He did not once wish for a sister, let alone one that looks so much like Dad. Reportedly, the nurse sought out Dad in the waiting room and said she did not even need to know his name because the baby looks just like him. Mom says I gushed out, like I could not wait to get here, in twenty maddening minutes to be exact. Such irony resides in this. I ravenously pushed my way into this world as if I needed to rush out of my warm, dark, watery bubble before it popped, and break through to the surface of air and bright lights and my mother's moaning, like an Olympic swimmer reaching for the gold. And why was I in a hurry, risking brain damage? Because it was out of my control as I was being dragged like the pull of the tide to a place I was not quite ready to go. Like so much of my growing up years, I felt I was being dragged by strong currents year after year to foreign beaches, because I never once felt that I was in control and I was afraid.

Fear was my constant companion for so many years. The fear of having to talk and let someone react to the sound of my voice.I did not utter a single word until I was three years old. Anna and Tony were not worried because they full well knew that I understood language. Psychologists have written that there are no memories recorded in our brains until we are five years of age. If that is true, then any amount of digging into my subconscious will prove fruitless. So I do not know why I chose not to speak. Maybe there was no need to talk. Maybe Mom was overzealous and did all the talking for me. Maybe I learned not to take any risks with language for fear of being misunderstood, something I always felt growing up. Maybe that thought is too sophisticated for a two year old.

Then there was the fear of choosing my own clothes to wear because I had not developed a comfortable style of my own. It was the fear of answering a question out loud at St. Agnes School; I preferred to not say anything and to allow Sister Eucharia and all of my third grade classmates to think

I was not smart. I just could not bear the sound of my own voice and the knowledge that everyone would hear it and just maybe be listening. The fear of trying anything new was a dragon with fire and brimstone, like riding a two-wheeler down the stony alley with a neighbor's hand holding the seat while she runs beside me, waiting for the instant she would let go. And I would fall, and then get back up with bloody knees, ironically determined to balance myself, while teeter-tottering on the edge of the cliff of fear. There it was, *determination,* like a tiny bud, which when given the elements it needs, will one day blossom.

Elementary school began in the first grade and ended with the eighth. The public schoolers called it Junior High. I called it a place of torture.

It is so remarkable that in the human condition, inside the fragile state of the heart, we tend to remember one of the horrid and hideous things that have happened to us more readily than all of the endearing, hilarious, tingling, soul-stirring, and breath-taking things put together. Like, what do I remember about eight years of wearing a maroon jumper, short sleeved tan blouse and navy blue knee highs? Oh, and I can't forget the beanie for my head, maroon of course. To this day, I will not wear the color maroon. It gives me pain. St. Agnes School was a living nightmare that translated to my younger sister, Diane. She must have seen the fear of a deer caught in headlights inside my eyes each day as I put on my maroon jumper; because when it was her turn to enter the heavy, wooden doors of the school building, she turned around and lunged out at Mom, holding onto her leg as if she were holding onto the trunk of a tree during a flood.(I have to note that years later when I was entering college, we had a horrendous storm called "Agnes" that caused substantial flooding in the Baltimore area, in fact Ellicott City Main Street, just a few miles from Catonsville, was under water.) Diane was screeching like an animal caught in the steel teeth of a trap. Mom was desperately trying to peel her tiny fingers off of her flesh. I was starting to feel sick at heart which caused those familiar waves of nausea to surge inside my acidic stomach. Like clock-work, when the *alarm* is wailing, the heavy set nun wearing yards of navy blue as vast as the sea, barrels out of the building, to rescue my mother. Diane's face is bloody red, her light brown corkscrews bouncing as Sister *Do As I Say* carries her inside, legs kicking. Mom just gets in her car and goes home. I'm left to face the executioners of my fragile self-esteem, alone. I walk the hallway, step by step, as cautiously as one who steps upon the African terrain and does not want to come face to face with a tiger or an elephant. Either you will get eaten alive or trampled to death. I enter the world of concrete walls. Not a word passes my lips. By the seventh grade, I had gone to the doctor's because butterflies resided in my stomach. I took tranquilizers just to get the courage to finish out the year. The doctor remarked that I was too young to have this amount of anxiety. He did not know that I had been engaged in combat these past seven years and I now had a severe case of battle fatigue. I had been fighting *fear* all my life. It was haughtily taking over my life, mocking me, accusing me, and making me feel guilty like I was stealing someone else's two molecules of oxygen, or I was eating a Tastykake that I didn't deserve to eat. I felt *less* than others. I remember sitting in the student lounge at Catonsville Community College and thinking, *that girl over there is homely looking, over-weight and slovenly, but she's eating and having a good time of it. So why can't I eat without that surge of nausea that starts the moment food touches my lips? I guess I don't deserve to eat like she does.* By that time I was eighteen. When was I going to feel comfortable being me?

So there I was in the first grade and I was accused of talking to the girl behind me. I had turned around to look at her because she poked my back, but remember, I was the girl who did not speak. The nun told me to come up to the front of the room. She then told me to turn and face the class. Then she punched me on the back. My face turned red, my eyes watered, and I was then told to sit back down. After that, I did not speak until the eighth grade, when I started having rebellious thoughts of tuning out the nuns, because soon I was going to high school. Apathy was my only defense. I stood right up to Sister Mary Patrick that year and told her I was *not* going to be in her Irish chorus for St,.Patrick's Day. She asked me why. I just shrugged my shoulders. Her face turned red with anger. I had to sit in the back of the room with the three "bad boys" after that. So it was the bad boys and I writing, while the rest of the class was singing, "*When Irish eyes are smiling . . .*" Also during my first year at St. Agnes School, I was told to go up to the fourth grade classroom, my brother's class. As I stood in front of all of those big kids, the nun started yelling at me to tell my parents that my brother is a slacker and a daydreamer, oh, and lazy too. Little did they know that Johnny has dyslexia, nor did they ever care to discover it. It wasn't until college that Johnny found the key to his reading difficulties: so much for a catholic education in the 1950's, one for which my father worked and sacrificed. I also remember being reminded by my teachers that I have a scar on my forehead. My first surgery was at six months of age, my second was at eight years. So I had to go to school with a bandage on my forehead and have the nun ask the nurse to come up and see it and to ask me questions. How did I know anything about it except that I did not want it pointed out. It was like wearing a flashing neon sign to school: *look at me.* Another *fond* memory was my father and I standing in line in the eighth grade classroom en route to receiving Johnny's report card. Other parents were in line in front of us and behind us. I don't know why I was there and not Johnny. Maybe he had pretended to be sick. When it was our turn, the nun raised her voice at my father and basically told him that his son was a lazy good-for-nothing. My dad's face was turning shades of red I never knew existed. He said he would talk to Johnny. Talk? Hell, no. He yelled at him and punished him for all the embarrassment he caused him. I remember thinking that my father should have yelled at the nun for disrespecting *him* and his family. Oh, I wished he had! And oh, I felt sooo badly for my father. She was belittling *my father*, the head of our family, a World War Two Veteran who almost lost his life fighting for the freedom of this nation. Her battle was with a 13 year old who had trouble reading! It was shameful. And it was hard to understand that my father had respect for her sisterhood, even if she did not deserve any. On the way home he appeared calm, but I knew he was furious, and it was only a matter of minutes before the volcano was going to erupt!

Dear St. Agnes School in Baltimore, Maryland in the town of Catonsville, within walking distance from my rowhome in Academy Heights! My saddle shoes (two toned oxfords, white and navy blue) slapped the pavement on Mt. DeSales Road every afternoon Monday through Friday. But the one day I remember is the day I heard two boys behind me, *Is it Charley and Joey?* I dared not turn around. My instincts told me to speed it up but don't run because that's an admission of fear. It was early 1960's and President Kennedy made me feel safe to live in America, anywhere but on this street at this time. Raucous laughter cracked and peeled the humid air as if it were an eggshell. Words hurt and become etched in your memory, like a spear hurled at an already shriveling sense of self-worth. *"Hey you, nigger, turn around."* My hair is kinky, thick, and curly. My lips are full. My skin is olive. I'm Italian. I should have turned around. Looked right into their eyes to see what cruelty looked like. But I felt it soon enough. Smacked me hard on the back of my head. I looked behind and didn't see the boys. There were trees and houses to hide behind. Then I saw it. A dead squirrel, a mangled paw dangling helplessly from a lump of gray fur stiff with dark blood. I could not hear my own screaming, only a ringing in my ears. It felt like slow motion, my skinny legs growing heavier and heavier as I raced up hill, and then downhill, my feet barely touching the ground. I rattled the gate, pushed the kitchen door open like a gust of wind, and quivered in tears to my mother to avenge me. Nothing was avenged because nothing was admitted. I hated myself for not turning around! I so wished that day would dissolve down the drain with the shampoo suds, and I dreaded to become the talk of the schoolyard the next day. My brother, Johnny ran out to the alley and yelled at the boys nonchalantly passing by to *leave his sister alone.* His voice was firm and deeper than usual, being 15 years of age. I was so grateful to him that monstrous day, but I don't think I even thanked him.

So the years of concrete walls and chalk dust were not my favorite. Still, I had to go to mass every morning because I took the early bus. Come on, how long does it take to drive one mile to school? Naturally, Diane, my cousin Nancy and I hid behind the wheels of a parked school bus, and naturally Sister Eucharia, all four feet of her, pointed nose and chin and all, found us and escorted us right up the concrete steps to the church. If we did not have our beanies, no matter, Sister pinned a Kleenex tissue on each of our heads with bobby pins she just happened to have in her pocket. In those days, no good catholic girl was seen in church without a head covering. Some women wore hats, some veils. Teenagers wore folded handkerchiefs and some even wore doilies. It was tradition. The mass was spoken in Latin and we each had "missals" which were prayer books with the mass printed word for word, one side of the page in Latin and one side in English. It was a challenge to follow along, so I spent my time staring at the light filtering through the stained glass, royal blue and ruby red and emerald green . . . There was a statue of Mary Our Queen, St. Joseph, and St. Agnes of course. The Stations of the Cross were hanging on the walls in raised marble relief, and the crucifix of Jesus with Him crucified was suspended above the altar. It was the focal point, larger than life. After my survey of all the statues, my next point of interest was looking at the backs of heads and watching them move. For that reason, I never sat in the front rows. Church was a huge part of my growing up years, six days a week during the school year, seven if you count Saturday confession. Nancy, Diane and I would walk up Academy Road or Mt. DeSales Road and of our own free will enter the church on our day off. We would line up along the wall and wait our turn. If we should hear the murmurings of someone inside the confessional, we would giggle without a sound. We knew each other was because our shoulders moving up and down and our faces enclosed in our hands was a dead give away. The church was quiet as a tomb, late afternoon sun illuminating a trail of dust from pew to window. Then we'd hear Father Bechtel slide shut the confessional window like he was viciously slicing it with a razor blade and we'd gulp. *Soon it will be my turn. Oh God, don't let me laugh any more. He might hear.* One time I forgot the Act of Contrition, *Oh my God I am heartily sorry for having offended you . . . uh . . . uh . . .* The priest kept looking at his watch, either bored or annoyed or both, and he curtly chopped the prayer to help me along. Sorry, my sins were not that exciting to hold his interest. It was always *say three Hail Mary's and two Our Father's.* So when I emerged from that dark ruby red cushioned cubicle that had a kneeler and a window screen with a sliding door that always scared you, not knowing exactly when Father would slice the silence and tilt an ear toward you, I would always look solemn, peeling apart the ruby velvet curtain. I then would kneel at the altar, silently reciting my penance, and would not get up until Nancy and Diane were finished. Upon leaving, we would remark that we felt so clean and so free. We practically skipped home. Within 24 hours, I was dirty again, having had fought with my mother or my brother, Johnny. *Darn. I have to go back there next Saturday!*

Eating lunch at school meant going to the closet behind us, the cloakroom, and getting our lunch boxes so we could eat at our desks. The room would then smell like bologna and peanut butter and tuna fish and chalk dust. In the first grade, I mustered up enough courage to tell Sister that I could not find mine. She found it for me but then put my face inside it. *"Is this your name?!"* After that, I made sure I found it on my own. It was a big deal to get to eat lunch inside the auditorium of the historically old gray stone school building. Long rows of folding tables and nuns patrolling our every move.

I remember one Friday during Lent when the nun came right over to me the second I unwrapped the waxed paper. There it was: bologna between two pieces of bread. She grabbed the meat with her fingers and threw it into the trash can. I was left with bread that had her fingerprints on it. That was one of the few times my mom was furious at a nun. She made a telephone call. When it comes to food, you do not mess with an Italian mother. I cannot remember if I ever told my mother about all the humiliations I had to endure and truthfully, I don't believe my mom would have done anything about it. What's the alternative? Go to public school? That was not an option.

So was it any wonder that in the fifth grade, the whole class applauded when Mark C. who was pushed into the blackboard by Sister, actually kicked her in the shins?! Maybe others felt it was funny. I felt avenged. It was worth all the times Mark kicked some of us in the shins on the playground. I guess he was practicing for his showdown with Sister. Funny, he was never suspended for kicking us . . . but not so when Sister got it. It was so significant to me that after forty some years, I still remember his full name.

But the place to which I always came home was 446 Greenlow Road, a corner rowhouse that connected to Palsie, my grandmother. Rose Marie Centineo Brocato, my mom's mom,wore a bandanna on her head and lit the oven with a match. Her hands were kneading the bread dough, rolling the biscotti dough, flattening pie crust, whipping the egg whites to peak for lemon meringue pie, stirring vigorously the egg and cheese, pounding the chicken cutlets . . . She had only basic ingredients but she knew *l'arte d'arrangiarsi*, as they say in Italia, "the art of making something out of nothing." She took scraps from the many blankets she had knitted and made another, giving it to me apologetically, *"You don't mind, do you?"* To me, it represents so much of her life as a widowed grandmother: something out of nothing. We call that *resourceful*.

I like to call it, *love*. There was nothing she owned or cooked or made that she did not share. Mom is just like that. Back then, neighborhood kids just had to wave, stop and chat, or ask a question. Some mornings, Mom opened the kitchen curtains to find Richard sitting cross legged on the sill. If I were so lucky to have a friend at school, I always brought her home to meet Mom. There was Mary T. and Rosemary P. during the

6th and 7th grades. In my neighborhood, I had Kathy E., Karen W. and Ann H., all who moved away by the time I hit high school. We were single friends. If I was with Ann, then Karen and Kathy were not with us, and so it went for each one. I was the common denominator. So I was never part of a group, except for the lunch table at Archbishop Keough, my high school that was in Baltimore City. Though we girls came from all over Baltimore and surrounding counties, my lunch table was girls from Catonsville for the most part: two Nancy M.'s, Dottie, Madeline, Margie . . .

It is an all girls school so I only attempted to be friends with girls. What did I expect when Cardinal Gibbons, an all boys school up the road from ours, had a dance and I was too shy to make conversation? I remember accepting a dance from a boy who probably couldn't get any girl to say yes. When he grabbed my hand, his was sweaty. I wanted to die. He bought me a coke and I hate soda. I was having a miserable time. I wanted it to be like in the movies or on TV: a really cute guy who can't take his eyes off of me and then we finally meet and the rest is dreamy history. I wanted other girls to stare at me in jealousy! I wanted to be prom queen one day! But mostly I wanted to dream about it, and I looked forward to the next episode of my *wouldn't it be loverly* life each night I closed my eyes. Pretty pathetic, I know, but it was *my* life and if I wanted to get through these years, it had to be spent in fantasy.

Somehow I was the girl most likely to get pushed in the hallway. At St. Agnes, there were the bony hands of Mary H. who repeatedly pushed me while in line behind me. In the brief months of attending Catonsville High School and my father beaming because he was saving a boatload of money, there was some black girl who pushed me in the halls. When I looked back, she and her group laughed at me. Naturally, that daily incident, compounded by the fact I had no friends here, and Chemistry was utterly impossible, I cried to my father to put me back in Keough, which is at present, Seton-Keough. I used to wear a wig of long straight brown hair one day and then reveal my own short curly brown hair the next, and then back to the wig. No one noticed. That said it all! So here I was crying to Dad, begging him to sweat it out, and to pay double the raised tuition, since he had to then start Diane as a freshman. He did. Just like he called the scout leader one evening and convinced her to let me join an already full enrollment of Girl Scouts of America. I was in it for one year : a banner full of earned badges and camping in the woods, and sewing together a sock monkey, and all. Then one day after school when I was descending the stairs of the old stone school building to get to the auditorium and join my troop, the cool girls asked me why in the world would I want to be a part of *that* group? I thought it was an invitation to join theirs. They shaved their legs and wore make up, even bras. So I came right back up the stairs and never went down them again at 3:00. I got to hang around the cool group at recess but that's all. They did all the talking and I did all the listening. Maybe I was the only one who did. I was friends with Linda G. when she was overweight in the eighth grade and still part of the cool group. The next year at Keough, she had drastically shed her pounds and acted like she didn't know me, though we had spent many afternoons at each other's house. I found out later that she was doing drugs and then I understood the glassy blue eyes and the bony frame. I started feeling sorry for her, and then all of my hurt feelings dissolved away. Sister Stanisia, my Home Economics teacher, with her short stature and apple cheeks, always told me to have confidence in myself. She used to say that I was pretty. *Who me?* I just did not see it. I spent most of that class ripping out the threads of my sewing. Sister ended up finishing my project, herself:a brown gathered skirt. I never wore it but I kept it for many years. It reminded me of Sister, one of the few nuns who meant something to me.

No matter how disappointing my school experience was, I could always count on my family to be there for me, even if we three siblings fought each other. It is *la mia famiglia* just the same. The coffee pot was always perking black; Mom was folding laundry on the kitchen table while her soap opera blared from the counter top. Always the smell of chicken or shrimp frying in Crisco; steak sizzling in the broiler, or a roast browning in the oven. My father sold meat for Auth Brothers to restaurants and hotels, so we had our supply as well. I was always the last one to finish supper when we had meat. It took me forever to chew it for some reason. I had no problems shoveling the shrimp into my mouth. We had plenty of food and company. Family always stopped by: Aunt Mary and Uncle Dominic, Aunt Anna and Uncle Joe, Aunt Theresa and Uncle Sam, Aunt Josie and Uncle Ernie, Uncle Frank and Aunt Ida. We were the center because Palsie, their sister, lived right next door. Some of my mom's family lived right in our neighborhood and to this day, they all live close : her sister Rosemary and Jimmy across the alley . . . her sister Franny and Dad's cousin Sal, down the street . . . . her brother Sal and wife Dottie next door to Franny. Aunt Mary was only three blocks away. She always visited us with jokes to tell and gum to give. We kids visited her when we trekked down to the playground at Christian Temple which was right by her house and was included in our neighborhood. Our pant seats were brown when we knocked on her door, because the slide, which stretched down a big hill, had a circular ditch of dirt at the bottom.

Uncle Frank always brought advice with him when visiting. Uncle Ernie brought boxes and boxes of ice cream.

He owned the *Tutti Frutti Ice Cream Company* on Caroline Street in Baltimore City, near Little Italy. Just about everybody in Little Italy knew Ernie as their godfather or their friend's godfather. Aunt Anna came with her talent of making the ordinary sound extraordinary, always having a story to tell and a laugh to share. Palsie, or Rose, brought her homemade pies and pizza bread and she always had someone's name on her tongue. This one and that one, and don't forget so-and-so, and what's-her-face . . . . Mom was famous for her apple pie and her buttery pound cake, not to mention the biscotti, in which everyone specialized. And so I grew up in a house with the Italian smells of basil, olive oil and garlic; the sounds of Italiano words thrown in here and there in any given conversation; a father who figured out solutions to all of our kid problems ; and a mother who tucked us in at night and read us bedtime stories, and who also figured out solutions to our kid problems, but always starting with, *what's the matter with you?* I was eight when Anthony Joseph Aquila, Jr. was born. Now there were four, but the difference was, nobody picked a fight with Anthony. He was the baby, and so adorable with golden curls, brown eyes and olive skin. On warm days, I would give him a bath in a plastic tub in the backyard. We couldn't resist and sometimes Diane and I would dress him up like a girl because of that sweet face and those bouncy curls. I think it convinced Mom to take him to Sal's Barber Shop to get a *big boy hair cut.* Years later, Anthony became a barber and he is now the *owner* of Sal's Barber Shop, having bought it from our disgruntled uncle.

My dad had given Sal Brocato a break when no one else would. He took out a loan so that Sal could open shop, taking the risk for my mom's brother. Tony, my dad, lived to see his namesake buy the shop. I look at it as God blessing Dad because of his generosity. There were times in the past that my father had made a few payments for Sal. Unfortunately, Sal had not shown much gratitude and is now combative towards Tony, Jr. All I can say is that we must all "work out our own salvation with fear and trembling." (Philippians 2:12).

We must be sober and diligent when it comes to following God's Word. When He looks upon us He sees our hearts, the naked truth. We cannot hide.

I always wanted an older brother who would look after me. Johnny was not that person. With each passing year, it became clearer that he resented me. Diane and I were kind of close. We shared the same bedroom, even the same bed for a number of years. But we are as different as the color black is to white. So I gravitated toward Anthony.

The age gap started to close when we moved to Deer Park Road. In the ranch home lived mom and dad, Anthony and I, at least for a little while until I married Danny.

Johnny moved there with his first wife. Diane moved back twice with her family. And we moved back once with ours. Dad and mom said the door was always open. We had all moved back to save money for a house . . . in Johnny's case, an education. It is never good to go back home, they say. I tend to believe they are right; however, I would love my own children to prove me wrong.

When my father died, the family started to crumble, pebble by pebble. Diane urged Mom to remodel and sell her house as quickly as possible. Mom refused to live there and moved in with her sister, Franny, next door. The house sits there on the hill, sterile, silent, and unloved. Branches have fallen off the trees from heavy winter snowstorms and from the gusty winds of spring. The new kitchen shines with granite countertops and stainless steel appliances, but does not smell like the kitchen on Greenlow Road, or like the kitchen it used to be. It smells new, that's all. Lamps turn on and off by a timer. The garage door is always closed. No car anymore. The mailman still delivers the mail in the mailbox across the street by the fence. Horses still hang their heads over the fence and whinny at him, as if to complain that things are just not the same. Where is that man who used to come to the mailbox in his slippers and robe? The man who rode his tractor, sometimes with deer at his elbow.

So when I think of what comforted me during those fledgling years, I think of Greenlow and the tiny rectangular kitchen with the black, creviced formica bar, the perking glass coffeepot, the chicken frying in olive oil, or the spaghetti sauce bubbling in the pot. Mom with her bandanna and Dad with his newspaper, *The News American,* and us with our catholic school homework.

There is a controlling spirit in my Italian family, inhabiting some of my aunts and a cousin or two. It must have originated from Uncle Frank who gushed with advice on parenting though he only had one daughter, Ann, and I don't think they ever bonded. Then there was Aunt Angel who never had a child but was bent on trying to control us by her "opinions" about children. I was judged on a daily basis by my aunts, if not by what I said then by what I looked like. My hair was wild and I mean frizzy out of control. Aunt Connie, my grandmother Palsie's sister, came to the house with a sure remedy of pouring Wesson Oil all over my head, wait twenty minutes, then rinse out. Was she making a salad out of my misery? Needless to say, it did not work. Once in my freshman year, I begged my mother to let me go blonde. So she peroxided my hair in the basement bathroom. Now I had carrot red hair that looked like a bush that needed pruning. Up the street comes Sal with scissors in his barber hands. He cut it so short that all I could think of was Mia Farrow married to Frank Sinatra with that little boy haircut. That was how I looked boarding the school bus the next morning. Sure, my natural brown color did not have far to go to outgrow the dreadful red. Still, it confirmed my belief that nothing I wanted to do or become in life was going to turn out. But then again, if my mom had taken me to a salon, I would have walked out a blonde. A blonde with very dark eyebrows, that is. Somewhere in the maze of class schedules; nuns who waited in corners by stairwells to grab you and check to see if your gray wool skirt was rolled up, or why else was it so short; and the chewing of pencils while taking math exams; there sprouted little green shoots of hope. Beer can rollers. And zillions of bobby pins to plaster down unwieldy bangs. Later, I was into braiding at night and wearing crimped hair by day. My hair consumed my high school years, leaving me feeling orphaned. *Why can't I have that silky London Look hair that dominates every page of Seventeen magazine*? I loved *The Beatles, Twiggy,* and *Jean Shrimpton.* It just wasn't fair.

Smoothing out my hair was so much work and still it did not look right, all dented and fluffy.It was difficult to fit it in with all the catholic school homework and my dad always yelling at me to turn off my light. Even if I were reading a book! Diane complained and dad just didn't want to hear it . . . again . . . *so shut the light right now!!!* How could I go to sleep when I hadn't whipped my hair into submission yet? Well there was always braids. In my junior year,my cousin Lois took me to Pikesville to a wig store where real human hair was sold wholesale. I was fortunate enough to have had won the Lion's Club essay contest on the subject of "peace." The prize: $100.00. Just enough money to buy me hair. I had to wear a headband to hide the seam but I didn't mind. I now had long straight brown hair way down my back at my will. My dad had his toupee and I had my fall(as it was called). Just like dad, now I had my very own styrofoam head. A year later, I ended up cutting my fall to shoulder length. The next year, I threw it in the trash can. I decided after graduation that my hair was part of who I am, after discovering that the opposite sex did not give one iota about the texture of my hair. I now had boobs and a butt and dates. I was so done with high school.

So I grew up in the comfort of my parents' love, home cooking, and a doting grandmother next door. Mornings were reborn with aromas of coffee, toast, and sweet cologne. Running water, toilet flushes, and banging doors . . . pots and pans, cabinet doors, and the Eye Witness News weather report . . . and we were out of there. Afternoons were met with relief, but with arms fully loaded with books. We hit the neighborhood on bikes or on foot in alleys with a basketball in hand. After dinner, we would hit the books, and as always, engage Mom as if homework is a team effort, or even a matter of parental ownership. *Mom, what is the word that describes doing something for your own good? "Expedient." Thanks!* Nights were tucked away by the wrapping up of the day's remains and the covers pulled up to our chins. We could hear the murmurings of the TV downstairs, and the running of toilet water turning on and off for no apparent reason. It was our lullaby.

We had no computer, no electronic games, no cell phones (what is texting?), no DVD player, nor VCR, only 6 channels on television (and color was a new phenomenon). our records were megatherian and carrying a whole stack of them made your forearm muscle ache. The record player needle was sensitive and invariably scratched the record and caused a skip or a stick in the sound. You'd have to run over and move it without scratching it some more. The hands of a brain surgeon . . . perfectly steady. But,what we did have was imagination, a few friends, bicycles, balls of all kinds, and two feet to take us just about anywhere, as long as we stayed in Academy Heights. I survived all of this plus years and years of dating the wrong boy until I met Danny Steinnagel. My father used to say, *Barbara, you expect a prince in shining armor to come to your doorstep???* And that is exactly what happened! Karen and Gregg brought him to my house one evening. I was having a *wine and cheese party/ prayer meeting.* And there he was, six feet two, platform sandals, cutoffs, and a full beard. It was 1977, what can I say? My hair was dark, curly, and wild, and when he touched it, saying he never met someone like me before with hair like that, I decided he was not the one for me. Two years later we were married. He did not know my hair was the reason I could not get a date in high school, and the reason why I was ugly and therefore painfully shy. Or was it?

When Kelley was one year of age, in 1991, Danny changed our name, all eight of us, to *Cook*, his birth name. His biological father, Tom Cook was in tears. His stepfather Ed Steinnagel, as well as his mother, Delores, and sisters, Bobbi and Julie, never spoke to us again. He tried to resurrect a relationship with them, but it only proved that it was long gone dead and buried. Their loss. Danny did what he thought was right, giving his only son his true blood name to pass on. Ed did not care that the children had his name at birth. He had told me so. Turned out, the only family member of his who loved him was his absentee father, Tom, who had issues of his own which could fill a book. It was one week before our wedding that Tom contacted Danny. They met in Salisbury, Maryland, hugged and cried and reconciled. Until Tom's death in the 1990's, we had a relationship with him as close as you can for someone who missed 20 years of his son's young life. My father, Tony, truly loved Danny as a son and Danny loved him as a father. He learned what it is to be a dad through him those 31 years of knowing him. Barbara and Danny married on June 30, 1979. By the following December, I was pregnant with Michelle Rose and it is here that my story as *mother* begins . . .

CHAPTER TWO

THE CRIB

Actually there were two, one bright yellow and antiquated, and one mahogany with spindle bars, a Jenny Lynd. Michelle Rose in one and Anna Maria in the other. A stately tree shaded their tiny bedroom in Lochearn, a Baltimore County neighborhood not far from the city but one in a forest of trees. The girls are 18 months apart and I remember Michelle pitter-pattering over to me as I held my newborn in my arms and I said, *Michelle, this is Anna your sister.* I also remember thinking that Michelle with her bouncy curls is just a baby herself and what did I do? Two babies in two cribs in a tiny house that looked like it belonged to *The Three Bears* . . . So how is it I had elected no drugs during the 35 hours of labor with Michelle and the 3 hours of pushing? Why is it I depended on ice chips and belly rubs given to me by two student nurses instead of drugs while in an even more painful labor with Anna? How was I so brave? In the absence of fear you will climb that mountain without looking down. Where did the fear go? It was behind me now because I kept on looking up.

When I was 21 and I still saw the world as a hostile place, my mother had asked me to go with her to a healing service at St. Timothy's Church on Ingleside Ave., about a mile from home. I had nothing to lose. I remember approaching the altar with trepidation in my heart and thinking it will beat right through my chest. Father Phil Zampino placed his hand on my head and told me that I did not have to be afraid any longer, that God was doing a great thing in my life. I was stunned! I did not know this man, nor did he know me. All that week, I read the Gospel of John, like he had urged us to do. The church was bursting at the seams with needy people, people who could not get in lined up outside the old wooden doors. They made an overflow room in the auditorium equipped with speakers. And the whole message? *Jesus loves you and He has come to give you abundant life.* Abundant life! That's what I wanted. So I went back each Tuesday night. Within two weeks, I realized I was not upchucking anymore first thing in the morning to start my day. My stomach was not tied up in knots. Something had released me from its tightfisted grip. Let go and got lost. My familiar companion who had cheated me out of all that is good and enjoyable in life had no more power over me. Fear had deserted me. I was left alone to live. But never alone.

During each labor and delivery experience with Danny by my side coaching me to exercise my calming breaths, I filled my thoughts with the Word of God. *"I can do all things through Christ who strengthens me."* (Phil.4:13). Danny read The Psalms to me for hours. I wouldn't let him stop. It gave me strength and confidence. It gave him a dry mouth I suppose. But he was more than willing to succor me. Other women were screaming for help. I was quiet, meditating on God's Word. I knew where my help was coming from! It was a good trade off for both of us.

Michelle was born coughing and clearing her own throat. Usually the doctor clears the infant's mouth with a sweep of his finger to help with that When Dr. Stasiowski placed the skinny long limbed body on my stomach, she just looked right up at me and stared, as if to say, *So you are my mother. Did you know that I can see through you to your soul?* That's exactly what it felt like. Michelle Rose was over 7 pounds and hypertonic. Stiff and tense. *Intense* is more like it. Can a newborn worry? Doctor Young, my pediatrician, recommended I exercise her legs each time I diaper her. So I was not the only one who needed to exercise after giving birth. She would look up at me with those dark deep-set eyes, studying me all the while.

Anna Maria was born plump at a little more than 9 pounds. Though labor was only 5 hours, it felt like another 35. Did I mention that delivery was like strapping a wild stallion to each leg and then slapping them on their behinds? Little did I know that less than 4 years later, I would deliver while *two* stallions were strapped to *each* leg and I would birth my son, weighing in at 10 ½ pounds and 21 inches in length. Dr. Stasiowski wondered where I had put him. Amazing.

What was it about *the crib*? I never wanted Danny to take it to the attic. We had moved to Academy Heights, my childhood neighborhood, though I had wished my parents had rented the 446 Greenlow Rd. home on the corner and then sold it to Danny and I who were going to be married two years later; but they did not know at the time that he was going to propose, and anyway there was the matter of Diane and John who had been married a few years already and she would have pitched a fit, so it wouldn't have worked out. We ended up buying our cottage cape cod in Lochearn, instead, about a month before we married. Just Danny lived there until the wedding but it looked like the slums and he and I did a lot of scrubbing on our hands and knees. How romantic! I think he had a single lamp, a small table and chairs, and a double bed,all from his mother, all antiquated, and I know how much Danny hates antiques. But hey, he bought us a house!

Later, we bought 6124 Regent Park Road, a middle rowhouse, no foyer, no fireplace, no bay window, but soon to be filled with lots of children and other people's children, as our home was the center of attention. Our backyard was tiny but no space wasted : a small garden, a Little Tykes sandbox shaped like a turtle, a three-sectioned swing set, a plastic pool,and a wooden playhouse with three windows and a doorway that Danny built. Oh, but not without Gene and Gary, neighbors, taunting him because I thought it too small and he immediately took it down and rebuilt it that same Saturday morning in Catonsville,Maryland.

Regent Park had an attic, unlike Cedar Drive in Lochearn in which the upstairs *was* the attic! When Danny climbed that pull-down ladder in the upstairs hallway, stealthily hoisted the crib up, and then shut the trap door, I had an unsettled feeling that I wore everyday like a heavy woolen coat on a 100 degrees humid Baltimore afternoon. It was just not right. Danny's mind was settled. We had Michelle, Anna, Danielle, and Timmy. He had a son. The night Danielle was born, we were shocked! It was an easy labor and delivery and I had a girl! We were thinking boy, so we named her after Danny nonetheless. Gary had brought over a few 6 packs of beer, I am told, and the two of them drank to the birth of yet another girl! Gary had three boys and now we had three girls. And they lived right next door. There were weddings to plan! The boys climbed the fence everyday to play with the girls. It just so happened that their last name was *Valentine.* How perfect . . . . but they moved away before the middle school years, all the way up to Allegheny County in the mountains.

So naturally when our son was born, Danny thought our nest, or quiver, was full.

But I was still dragging around that woolen coat and my posture was starting to slouch, as if a heart could do that . . . slouch? I wanted that crib brought back down from that dark place of unloved and forgotten things. So I did what any woman would do in such a desperate situation. I literally wrestled Irish Danny one night until I wore him down and Alyssa Kathleen was born on *his* day, St. Patrick's Day. It had been a rough pregnancy. I was hospitalized that summer during my first trimester. We had no air conditioning and the rowhouse became a green house. Instead of plants, I was growing a child. The rainforest had nothing over us. The tomato plants were climbing the front porch, heavy laden with the plumpest reddest tomatoes we had ever seen. It was a fertile time, but I could not still the tempests of nausea raging inside me. The doctor would not release me until we had air conditioning. So my dad immediately bought us a large window unit and Dan installed it in our living room which would cool the entire first level. We could all sleep in that room if we had to. Before that, Danny would come home from carpentry with dirt on his face and have to wash the dishes that filled the sink enough to sink a ship. He had to wash diapers and change a few. And worse of all, he had to put up with moaning that serenaded him with my every breath. And guess who bathed the three little ones every night? Michelle was eight at this time and she probably helped him. Alyssa was born a happy baby! I could snap a picture of her at any time. Always smiling!

Danny was happy too! I felt good again and I could take care of our five children, no sweat.

Michelle Rose was 10, Anna Maria was 9, Danielle Christine was 6, Timothy Daniel was 4, and Alyssa Kathleen was 2 when Kelley Simona was born on June 26, 1990. When she was 8, I added *Toni* as her first name in order to honor my father. (He was seriously ill with kidney problems due to his heart medicine). Eighteen months after Alyssa's birth, Danny did not get the chance to hoist that crib back up into the attic.

It was still occupied. So . . . And what about the other crib? The yellow one was defunct because there was talk in the *baby circle* that the old cribs with the wide slats and wider spaces between, could be the cause of crib death. So naturally, I tossed that crib out. Just like when my mother had called me one sunny day in June and told me that the10 pounds of Red Delicious apples that I had just bought were tainted with a poisonous pesticide. At that time, the word *organic* was foreign to me. So without hesitation, before I even took another breath, those apples were tossed into the trash can by the gate near the alley. Not to mention the can was quite full already because of the full set of Club aluminum cookware(I had received at my bridal shower) that mom told me to toss because traces of aluminum had been found in Alzheimer patients. All on a sunny day. Of course, since then this has been disproved. So when Danny came home from carpentry with dirt on his face, he lifts up the lid to throw away a little trash bag from his truck and . . . . *WHAT THE HECK!* Oh, and by the way, those allegations against those apples proved to be false also. The bottom line: I wanted to make sure my children were safe from all harm. Another bottom line: I listened to mom without question. Simona (as she wanted to be called for the first three years of school) was my last baby even though Tim was still begging for a brother. The crib was now buried in the attic. I was 40.

Chapter Three

DIAPERS

Palsie, my grandmother, told me to call a number for free advice. I called the psychologist and she simply said in an upbeat voice, "Michelle will give up her diapers when *she* decides." Oh, so now I have to wait upon the will of a 3 ½ year old and I still have three in diapers! I felt like saying, "Are you kidding? You have degrees in psychology and you are agreeing with the decision of a three year old knowing she has a bad case of diaper envy?" I hung up after muttering a *thank you*. Thanks for nothing! When still living in Lochearn. I packed the entire house myself even though I was starting my second trimester pregnancy with Danielle. Michelle seemed oblivious to the fact that it was time to use the potty. I resorted to spanking because I did not know what else to do. I remember spanking her lightly but somehow the diaper pin opened and braised her tender skin. Now I was sobbing and hugging her tightly, telling her I am sorry! Danny was working overtime (overtime was becoming an expected addition to his paycheck), and I was still in my *first trimester 24-7 nausea marathon* hoping it will soon end. And Michelle had been marching through the house dropping a trail like Hansel and Gretel, only it wasn't breadcrumbs. Anna was screaming for her "bottle" which was myself, because I believed in nursing all of my children. That's when I spanked and that darn pin opened. I guess you wonder why I used cotton diapers, thick and heavy when wet. I had believed they were kinder on the skin, but then why was I going through one tube a week of diaper ointment? The cloth diapers required a dumping into the toilet, a pre-soak in bleach in the washer, and a full cycle hot wash using baby detergent. This was daily. So the diaper pin was not to be trusted! After that, I was always checking the pins on each of my babies like I had OCD. It was the same way when the bassinet was in our bedroom. Every hour I lay my hand on our baby's back to feel the gentle rippling motion of breathing. *Thank God the baby's still breathing!* Danny said I was not going to make it if I don't relax more. Relax and trust God.

When Alyssa was born we could afford to buy the plastic kind, like Pampers. Wow! I thought I was Albert Schweitzer in the thickets of the jungle discovering a new way to to help out the natives! They kept the baby drier and they brought me back to "civilization." No wonder Alyssa, my fifth, was always so happy!

We moved into Academy Heights on Regent Park Rd.in December, in fact it was one week before Christmas. My Aunt Sarafina was our agent and she had arranged our two settlements in one day. Smart. Michelle and Anna were with our friends Mary Jo and Chris who actually volunteered. Because the day swirled like a tornado, we did not have time to eat, let alone think. The movers piled all of the boxes in the unfinished basement that reeked of cigarette smoke.(After stripping the slum-like doors and refinishing them, the basement would be next on Dan's priority list.) Upon picking up the babies, Michelle 3 ½ and Anna 1 ½, we learned that they both had a bad case of diarrhea. Okay. We could handle that if only we knew where the diapers were in that Grand Canyon of boxes! I was as upset as if it had been The Ark of the Covenant buried in a crate God only knows where. Indiana Jones had nothing on me! While Danny was hastily setting up cribs and the babies were screaming, I was tearing through boxes to find help for my precious babies. Looking back, I just wish I had done it with a better attitude. To me it was a sign that we had made a mistake. We shouldn't have bought this house. What were we thinking? Things are never the same when you go back to your childhood neighborhood. As we say in Italia, *mai e poi mai* (never ever) will I think that it could be. It was after 10 o'clock at night and I started to cry right along with Michelle and Anna. Danny's exact words were: "I'm working as fast as I can!!! Now where are those screws?"

That summer on June 12th, Danielle Christine was born. Though I had again elected natural childbirth, her birth of over 8 lbs. was relatively easy. I was sitting up and actually having conversation during most of the labor. My neighbor Linda, a nurse and mother of the three little boys next door, said she felt like we were talking to each other over the fence. I still had to face the horses during delivery, but that part is always the shortest length of time, so bearable. Danielle was born quiet. Not good. Dr. Stas said not to worry. It's just that the umbilical cord is knotted and is now around her neck. No problem. He quickly loosened it. He said it was a wonder that she was fed in utero. Our miracle baby! Of course the nurses snatched her away to check her out. On March 5, 1982, two years before, Anna Maria was born after an excruciating labor. At a birth weight of over 9 pounds, I felt contractions that much harder. After her plump little body entered the world, the nurse put her immediately into an isolette because the larger infants lose their body heat more rapidly. When the nurse wheeled her into my room, I could not hold her, only put my hand through the circle to touch her. Danny could not visit because he was taking care of baby Michelle,18 months old. I remember grabbing the arm of a nurse and asking her to sit down and talk to me. She said she did not have the time. When she saw the tears welling up in my eyes, she reconsidered. Just for a few minutes, but I was grateful. Anna took to nursing, unlike Michelle. I had to be trained by the nurse and then I had to train Michelle. I suppose she was my only baby who did not suck her thumb in utero.

So now we were living in a house I called a *mistake* and we had three in diapers, cloth diapers that is. I was OCD again, with safety pin checks and breathing checks. It was seriously time for Michelle to give up her diapers. Dr. Young told me to let her clean up after herself when she messes. Right! Pampers no longer fit and she was wearing *training pants.* Just like *training bras,* I had no clue for what I was training her. "Pull Ups" were not invented yet. Hell, I should have invented them! The words of that psychologist were taunting me. But I have to admit, Michelle taught me something back then: nothing can come against the human will and succeed. And *free will* is a gift from God so who am I to expect her to give it back even for a few minutes?

It was an eventful week. My children had playmates over, nothing unusual except that my neighbor brought along her best friend's child, a little girl. She, herself, had two boys and my girls mostly played with boys at their young age. I just happened to leave the action in the backyard to check on Danielle sleeping in the bassinet in the living room. And then I saw it. A blanket was over her head and a little girl was sitting on the bottom step looking sheepish. I rescued Danielle and escorted the little one out. "Jealousy," my neighbor said. Yep. That's what caused Cain to slay Abel, the only two brothers on earth, as written in Genesis.

Later that week, Danny discovered he had a double hernia and needed an operation.

That little injury at work that he did not report turned out to be a big deal. It was during his recovery period at home that the lesson began. Knowing that I had miserably failed at potty training thus far, Danny decided to show me that it is not that hard "Consistency is the key." I was thinking, *we'll see who is the more stubborn.* But I said, "You're right. Go for it." Oh, and I might add, Dan got a little cocky and pushed it further. He said, "Just give me one day!"

Danny, walking bent over with pain, took Michelle, bouncing curls and all, to the bathroom. He sat her on the potty seat that was attached to the toilet. He gave her books to look at and walked away. You could hear the flipping of pages and then the slam of dropped books on the ceramic floor. I checked on her. She told me Daddy won't let her get up. Michelle was obedient and continued to sit there. So determined was Danny that he insisted he give her lunch on the potty. I humored him. Each of my children gave up nap time at two years of age. But this must have been exhausting for little Michelle. I found her with her head resting on the window sill beside her. She was sound asleep. My heart went out to her, but Dan's determination was rock-cliffed and relentless. What he did not realize was so was Michelle's. It was getting near 5 p.m. and Danny was still visiting her with his pep talks and I was still resisting releasing her. Finally at 5, Danny gave in. "*Take her off. Maybe she doesn't have to go*", he said. I was so happy to get her up. I put lotion on her bottom and gave her a big kiss for trying. As soon as she was standing with her training pants on, she released it. At the tender age of three, she proved her determination was much greater than a man of 31 years. Danny had to laugh! How can a body that small possess an iron will like an Amazon? Dan was resolute but Michelle was unyielding in her quiet way. She clearly confirmed what the phone psychologist had told me.

"But when *will* she be ready?" I ask while cleaning her up and hearing infant Danielle crying and wondering what Anna has gotten herself into. Meanwhile, Danny had a month recovery ahead of him and no workman's compensation or sick pay. What we did have were meager union comp. checks and Mom and Dad who brought over bags of food. Even Aunt Angel and Uncle Lou brought over a bag or two. We've always trusted in the Lord and this was no exception. Danny was able to return to work two weeks earlier than the recommended six week recovery. Michelle finally gave up her *training pants* at the age of four. She and Anna started using the potty at the same time. I suppose Michelle saw that, naturally, greater attention was given to those in diapers. Anna and she were like twins in stature, and I also suppose she saw herself as no different from her sister. So when Anna was on board, so was Michelle. Now why couldn't I figure that one out sooner? Anna was such an agreeable child that I could have started potty training her at 18 months. As we say in Italia, *idiota!*

Chapter Four

BED SHUFFLE

Tom Cook had saved some furniture for us from Falls Village, Connecticut where his mother, Grace, had just passed away. We had slept in those twin beds when we had visited Grace for the second time, that time without her and with baby Michelle. Grace was in the hospital and refused prayer with us, saying "It's not my time yet!" We had traveled there so she could see her great grandchild. She said she never thought she'd be a grandmother, "and now you have made me a great one." She spoke in a gravelly voice and she looked like a shriveled dwarf, the bed swallowing her up. Danny and Tom arrived a month later from their New England trek and unloaded the furniture, the twin poster beds among the heap in the truck bed. "Junk," Tom said. To me, they were antiques. Years later, the veneered maple was peeling away from the headboards and we could not find the missing oval piece that fit on the top of one poster. But they looked like they belonged in our girls' bedroom. We had yet another bed in there that had a tall dark mahogany headboard and it looked like Goldilocks had slept there. We were a house of curls except for Anna and Tim with their straight thick hair. Of course, Danny didn't count because he was quickly becoming more bald. With every birth, he lost more hair. Still, the straight hair gene comes from him. He has hair everywhere except the top of his head. Every once in a while, he would surprise us by secretly shaving his beard that had kept him incognito since I had met him. I almost did not know who he was! I thought it unfair to not reveal his true face until we had been married with several children. The children were suddenly insecure and felt timid approaching him for an embrace. After reassuring them that this is indeed their daddy, Danielle said in her quiet voice, "I want my old daddy back." So did I. It was hard getting used to a different face again and again.

The tiniest bedroom was the nursery. From there you could hear the neighbors as plain as if they were in that room. Our babies adjusted to noise from the very beginning. Noise was always a part of our decor just like the wood floors and ceiling fans. When Kelley was born, the phone machine next door in their smallest bedroom would constantly be recording messages of *where are you* and *meet me here* and *meet me there.* It was not unusual for the couple next door to leave their home dressed in black suits and carrying brief cases at 12 a.m. The next morning their car would be caked with mud. Naturally, I could not wait to move. Since Linda had moved, nothing but odd had moved in. The woman who had bought it decided to rent it out. Twice now, it had been rented to what appeared to be drug dealers, a prosthetic leg and a wooden cane tapping up the sidewalk regularly for a visit. The little dog next door would show his teeth and growl every time. Dogs and cats can sense when things are just not right.

To make room for our still growing family, we had to buy two sets of bunk beds.

At first we put one set in the smallest room and there slept Michelle and Anna. The next set was in the middle bedroom with Alyssa at the bottom and Danielle at the top. Timmy had the "three bears" bed with the high headboard my sister Diane had given us. The dresser was a hand-me-down from Sarafina, in which the drawers promptly fell apart after a few month's use. "Junk," Danny said. But Danny fixed what little track was left on each drawer so they could open a little less wobbly. The chest that came with it was no better. Michelle and Anna inherited that one. My father said he never saw two people who moved beds like we did. During those ten years living in Academy Heights, it was like we were always moving in and never settled. Dan and I would discuss bedrooms and chests over our Saturday morning cups of coffee. Alyssa was out of her crib and I was due to deliver Kelley in June. Alyssa's birth was a breeze. She was coming out of the birth canal as I was heaving from nausea. I did not even have to push. That's just like her. She could not wait to be born. When she was five, she would randomly burst out with *I love life* as naturally as one inhales and exhales. Kelley's birth was not quite as easy because I was just plain exhausted. I remember telling Danny, *I can't do this anymore. I want to get off this bed and go home now.* Already Danny, in his head, was making plans to see a doctor about a vasectomy! Kelley Simona was born over 8 pounds like Alyssa but I had to do some serious pushing. With Kelley in my arms, I thought about how that same little face was born all over again, and how beautiful she is just like her sisters and brother, and how are we going to arrange the beds *this* time? Tim had the double bed that used to be Danny's when he was a teenager. Old, dark and ugly, given to us by his mother. He finally had a bedroom to himself, the tiny room. But after two months of the bedside bassinet, Kelley needed the nursery and her own crib. So it was time to go bedroom moving again! Danny was always running up and down the attic steps (which was a pull down ladder in the hallway) in his untied work boots, storing beds and cribs piece by piece, and then taking beds and cribs back downstairs again piece by piece. So the smallest room was again a nursery.

After much configuration and consideration, the resolution to our problem of fitting six children into two small bedrooms became quite clear. We had to give up our master bedroom and take the middle room. Upon entering our *new* bedroom, you could only take two steps and you would hit the side of our queen sized bed. My dresser is a triple size so we had to walk sideways to get to the rest of the room. Danny's chest was in the corner by the windows and he did not quite know what space to stand in when dressing in the morning. Forget the vanity I got from Grandma Cook's estate. It too had fallen apart and I no longer had room for it anyway. "Junk." My father had suggested we put both bunk beds in the master bedroom. It looked like a dormitory and most nights it sounded like one. Of course, the double bed had to be stored in the attic again. At that moment, I remembered when Danny hoisted both cribs up into the attic and beamed, he's sighing and grunting that he has to keep pounding those stairs with headboards "Now we're done. Don't need these anymore. I've got my son!" Now two babies later, and box springs in his arms. If I could have helped him, I would have. As God as my witness, I was always pregnant, or nursing, or holding a crying baby in my arms. When Danny was shuffling beds, I was shuffling children in and out of rooms so they would not be in his way. Sometimes Dad and Mom would be there to give us ideas or to cheer us on, or just to laugh at us I suppose. But I think they admired our spirit. We loved bringing home the new baby, all six times. It was another miracle with which we were blessed. And another challenge. Which beds in which room?

So, we had Timmy, Danielle, Anna and Michelle in bunks in the biggest room. We had Alyssa in one of the poster twin beds in that same room. When it was time for Kelley to leave the crib at age two,(each one had adventures of climbing out and falling by that age), I had decided that because Michelle was in middle school, she needed a room by herself to do some serious studying. So guess what pair of steps were creaking again and whose boots were still untied?! Danny resurrected that double bed again and put it in the tiny room. In the bunk bed room, we put Kelley in the *same* twin poster bed as Alyssa. We had no room for another twin. In fact, Kelley's little white chest we had gotten from somebody (I can't remember who) was in the hallway. *The three bear's* bed was in the attic with the two cribs, the porta-crib, the changing table, and the high chair. My babies were growing up! If only we had room in which they could continue to grow! When Kelley was one year of age, we began our journey to search for a larger house. This meant piling all eight of us into our mid size station wagon and canvassing Catonsville for one of those historically old homes off of Edmondson Avenue. Every offer we made was rejected. Finally, we headed out to Carroll County and come to find out, Danny said he always had his heart set on moving out there one day. After two years of traveling miles and miles in our new red Caravan minivan, all eight of us with seven seatbelts, two children sharing one belt, Danny's *one day* had finally dawned in the country. More on that later.

Chapter Five

STRESS AND NATURAL THINGS

According to my brother Anthony who happened one evening to be driving down Route 40 in Catonsville, a young man in his early thirties was burning rubber on foot, *and was that steam coming out his ears?* His long hairy arms were furiously swinging like an ape in heat. Who was this man? Upon a second glance . . . *MY God, it's Danny!*

Neither Dan nor I can remember what was said between us to have put him into such a frenzy. Whatever it was, he walked it off which I think is a smart thing to do and I highly recommend it . . . My reclusive neighbor next door, Julie, gave me a relaxation tape after hearing me say I get chest pains sometimes. She was worried that I never get out beyond the backyard. But she had only herself to take care of. I had 7 people depending on me to: cook their meals, wash their clothes, balance our budget, make all the business calls, make all the visits to the pediatrician with preschoolers and an infant in tow, dry all the tears, administer all the medicine, attend all teacher conferences, clean the entire house, settle arguments between siblings, feed their friends and watch them too, dress each one for Sunday morning church (including Danny), and wash 6 heads, cut 6 bangs, trim 6 heads . . . . need I go on? I also had to prepare my Sunday School lessons to which I was committed for 26 years. Did I mention I had to change all the beds weekly, and you know how many there were! So I took the tape and after the last dish was dried (we did not have a dishwasher until later), I lay on the couch in the living room while Danny played with the children in the backyard. It was summer and we still had hours of daylight. I must say it did help me and I highly recommend it. The soothing voice told me to imagine each part of my body just melting away into the ocean. I felt like I could just float away. It is amazing how the mind controls the body. After the tape, I would drink a full glass of water, do some stretching, and then head out into the neighborhood for a brisk walk in the heat. When I would get to Davidov's, the corner drug store that sold all kinds of crap that we loved like cheap nail polish, bubble gum cards, penny candy, and sodas, I rested on the curb and watched the cars go by. I'm sure neighbors saw me and wondered why, but that curb felt so good; like when I was a young girl and felt so independent by walking out and being alone somewhere, just sitting on the hill at Mt. De Sales Academy, which was the crown of our neighborhood. Looking down at the rooftops I felt on top of things.

Now Danny was the sole provider and I did not go back to work until Kelley was one year old. I took a teaching position at Catonsville High School at night from 5 to 10 on Monday and Wednesday, teaching hoodlums American and British literature. I could write an entire book about that, but I continued with this job for 6 years until a female student punched me in the chest,and I fell into the desks onto the floor. I had on a long pencil skirt and my movement was limited. She grabbed my hair and started dragging me. It took three of my male students to release the grip of her fingers and then she bolted out the door. She had refused to keep quiet during an exam, so I had pulled her paper. She cussed me out and refused to go to the office. Then the real drama began . . . I asked for the police and I filed charges. In preliminary court, she and her mother lied. In court, the judge slammed his gavel and said, "No teacher should ever have to go through this." The Baltimore County Board of Education had recommended votech school. The judge said he was sending her to a detention center on the Eastern Shore for two years. Two hefty guards snatched her away, one at each of her shoulders. Before I could blink an eye, she was gone. My students missed me and wrote me notes. My children begged me not to go back. Danny asked me not to go back. I had a chest contusion and Baltimore County Schools still refused to hire a guard for the night school. I did not go back.

So Danny continued as the sole breadwinner until I started substitute teaching and I became a little bit of a help. I needed a job with flexibility since I still had all of my duties at home and whatever it took to raise my family. Danny cut the grass and shoveled the snow,which included the parking spots in front of our house that anyone could park in. He built us a deck, updated the kitchen, painted walls like crazy, and finished off the basement. He also did all of the grocery shopping those 10 years at Academy Heights so I did not have to bring all the children with me. I still had three babies at home while the other three were at school. Even two babies, even one baby, was too much for me at the grocery store. The few times I shopped while Danny was at home because he was too tired to go, I could hardly make the turns with the heavy laden cart. And it took me hours. Dan called me *Alice*. You know, the one who fell into the hole and took those funny pills. I was lost in aisles of cans and boxes.

Stress comes with parenting and surprisingly, it is always the little things that rocked our world back then. Spill a glass of milk and the whole dinner is ruined. Pull a neighbor's flowers from her front garden and you get a lecture, a spanking, and have to ring the doorbell and confess. No wonder Michelle convinced Anna to confess to what she did not do! Refuse to make your bed or to fold the laundry or to leave it there and not put it away, and *you are grounded!* But the *big* things? No sweat! Michelle stopping the glider swing by extending her skinny little leg? *Non c'e problema*! Danny kept coaxing her to stand on it when she sat in the kitchen insisting she could not. *Just try,* he coached her like she was contending for the Olympic gold and just had to get back out there. You cannot talk a broken leg into pretending it isn't. So we packed the children into the van and headed for St. Agnes Hospital. Dr. Mejia saw us there and spoke to someone so that we would be seen *pronto*.

Michelle was fitted for a cast and left the hospital looking like a thunder cloud. She regarded her crutches as leprosy, and instead scuttled around the house like a crab. My neighbor, Laura, whose son, Louie, was in the glider with Michelle, insisted that she pick up Michelle daily, wheelchair and all, and transport her in her van to kindergarten at Westowne Elementary. Her teacher, Mrs. Mitchell, insisted she should not drop out, even though at that time it was not mandatory to attend. I remember the wheelchair being strolled down the alley by Mrs. Mitchell and a whole troop of 5 year olds on a field trip to neighborhood playhouses to reinforce their "carpentry unit." We had that wooden playhouse in our yard and the class came to the fence to take a peek . . . Now I had two in casts. Two months before Michelle broke her leg, she and Anna had baby Danielle on the bed with them and she fell over the edge breaking her baby wrist. Michelle was 5 ½, Anna 4 and Danielle 20 months. I was soon to deliver Timmy, my 10 ½ pound son, and here I was at The Emergency holding my broken baby. A few days before, Danielle and I were standing on the front cement porch looking up at Danny who was on the roof surveying the broken slates. Danielle pushed through the porch gate and started tumbling down the concrete steps as I started screaming and Danny started hustling down the ladder, almost falling. She was cut on her face near her nose and blood was dripping onto her playsuit. Immediately, I transformed myself into the nurse mode. After cleaning, bandaging, and holding her, she calmed down, and pretty soon acted like it never happened. So when I appeared at The Emergency with Danielle, her face bruised and her wrist swollen which proved to be broken and a cast was put on, the nurse gave me a dark look and asked me a lot of questions, like, "Do you get angry quickly because of your hormones, being that you are pregnant?" Danny was still at work. I knew I could handle it alone and told him so. No sweat! It was many years later, in fact twenty, that Michelle confessed that it had been no accident. She and Anna were sick of her and just pushed her over. Whose idea was it? We reap what we sow. Yes, Danielle would cry. I wonder why! Was it because she was the third girl and the older two would not include her? Was it because we had made such a big deal about finally having a boy after three girls? Or was it because she could not hear out of her left ear and none of us knew, not even Dr. Young. She would come home from first grade, throw all of her notebooks at my feet in the kitchen while I was making dinner and needing to attend to nursing Kelley. She would stomp her feet and cry hysterically that she *cannot do this!* When I sat her down to go over the homework, she would cover her ear and turn away. That was a clue I did not pick up on. She was covering only her right ear, her *good* ear. By the third grade, her teacher tested her for learning disabilities because she was not picking up reading. No disabilities noted. We signed her up for a summer reading camp that used signing to help with reading comprehension. That was like a sign to us but we did not pick up on it. When she took the standard routine hearing test at school, the technician notified me. *Such a discrepancy between the right and left. See a doctor.* Dr. Cosentino is her ENT doctor now for these past 16 years, placing a tube in her left ear and puzzling why she has not outgrown this problem of fluid. We can put satellites and space stations into the dark, lifeless abyss of the outer atmosphere, but no one knows how to permanently solve the problem of fluid in one's ear. So we dealt with it in hope and prayer, as we do to this day.

You can tell a child not to run but you might as well tell a bird not to fly. Alyssa ran and tripped, striking her chin on the edge of a wooden step. I took her to my neighbor two doors up who was the only nurse left on the block, and she said to go to the hospital. It was Sunday morning and her pretty little dress was spotted with blood. She was trying to smile but she now had two pairs of lips. We called Miss Ann across the street and headed out. It took an orderly, Danny, and I to hold her still while the doctor stitched her chin closed. She had even been in a straight jacket which she wiggled out of, jumped off the table, and hid under a stainless steel cart. It did not shake me. I knew that if I wasn't calm, she would never be. I talked her through it and the doctor was able to stitch a clean edge. And there was Timmy who was told not to stand on Ibrahim's skateboard. So he thought about it and compromised. He sat on it. Our sidewalks had settled and he hit a rise in the concrete. The skateboard smacked him and he came home crying with blood streaming down his neck. He now had two pairs of lips. And low and behold, Virginia came over frantically one afternoon holding Ibrahim by the hand and he looked up at me crying with two pairs of lips. I told her to close his chin with the clean white cloth I gave her and

Danny and I drove her to the hospital. She had come to the right house. We had become experts in this field.

So why did the kids say, "Mom, you get upset over spilled milk! You act like it's the end of the world!" I contemplated this lately. What was in that glass of milk that pushed me over the edge again and again? It was all of the frustrations and tribulations of bringing children into the world and their sweet little faces looking to me to make everything right even if it was out of my control. It was not wanting to ever disappoint them or let them down when I knew deep down in my soul, that I had disappointed myself. Who doesn't want to be the perfect mother? The fact remains that none of us is nor could we ever be. So what did I see in that puddle of milk? That we all make mistakes and are less than perfect, even when we follow the best laid of plans. I used vinyl on the table instead of cloth. The youngest wore bibs. I made casseroles often, one dish meals that were economical and it avoided reaching across the table for this dish and that. Still the milk spilled. It would not have been dinner without it. Still life happens in ways you have not planned or wanted. So you get the dishcloth and you wipe it up, hoping it does not stain, does not leave a scar, one in which you spend most of your adult life trying to get rid of. And still life surprises you with moments so tender and sweet that if you live to be 120, it will still warm your heart and renew your faith in love. Even in the most exasperating of circumstances, there is something precious to be gleaned.

When we lived in Lochearn in our tiny cape cod and Michelle was soon to be born, a noise awakened me, like that of flapping wings. I thought maybe I had been dreaming of angels and sometimes I know dreams are so real you can hear them. When I looked straight ahead at the window, I saw the outstretched wings. It was either batman or just a bat. I woke up Danny. *Is that on the outside or inside?* "Quick! Hide your head under the sheet! I don't want it to go for your hair!" he urged me. Remember my bushy hair? I still had it. Danny opened the door and shook the white shears at the window. It flew out and right into the next bedroom, the nursery. *Thank God the baby isn't born yet.* I was emotional, frantic really, and I blame it on hormones. I cried and begged Danny to call his step-dad,Ed.It was 2 a.m., but he did. Of course his step-dad was no help, and I don't know what I expected, maybe that he would rush over here for emotional support? I shut myself into the bathroom just like Danny told me to do. He closed the door himself, maybe to protect me or maybe to get rid of me? He stood by the nursery door and counted how many seconds it took for the bat to circle the room. Then on the third revolution of this hideous creature, which is my worst nightmare, a mouse with wings, he swatted it to the floor with a broom. He banged it at least 20 times. Then he put it out in the street until tomorrow. The next day, it had been eaten by who knows what and was all but gone. Danny was my hero and it made me love him that much more. I knew from that night on, that no matter what the danger, Danny will protect me and our family to be. No matter what it takes.

I thought I would be brave also so that one morning when I was about 8 months pregnant, and I cleverly put on a Danny's yellow rain slicker and rubber boots, and my yellow Rubbermaid dish gloves, and held a broom in my hand. The trusty broom, the bat killer. I opened the bedroom window and whacked the hornet's nest that was woven into the upper corner and had prevented us from ever opening that window. Nothing like the sweet smell of summer air, a blend of blossoms and newly mown grass. And nothing like the drone of an army of hornets swarming at you. Nothing like whacking a nest with all of your might and only thin flakes chip off. I slammed that window shut! By God's providence that protects foolish people, only two bees were buzzing inside the room. I shut the door and declared war on them both. I smashed them to smithereens. Then I started to shake. Post-war trauma. Danny scolded me and hugged me, and kept repeating, *What were you thinking?* I just could not clearly answer that question. I guess I was mustering up bravery for things to come.

As soon as we had moved into 6124 Regent Park Road, I heard a noise downstairs early one morning. I was near my time to deliver Danielle and Michelle was only 3 ½, Anna 2. I stealthily descended the stairs and there it was! A big, black crow treading on my brand new camel-back sofa with Queen Ann legs. I ran back upstairs and shut the girls into their bedroom, warning them to not *dare* step foot out of there until Mommy gets the creature downstairs out of the house. They did not budge; I did not even hear anything upstairs. I called the guy next door who was 18 and asked him to come over even though he has never met me but I am in distress and can he help me? Stuart came over, tanned and very blond, and very young and introduced himself. I looked like I had just rolled out of bed because I had. He opened all the windows and doors and swore the crow would leave. He swatted at the curtain with a broom and when that creature flew out at him, he jumped back and yelled. I screamed. Stuart laughed and said, "See, it flew right out the door." We quickly closed all the windows and doors and that was the beginning of a long friendship. Stuart and his parents, Willa and Gene, were country people from West Virginia. They climbed on top of a picnic table to reach the rickety remains of a back porch in order to enter the house. When Danny talked about building us a deck, you would have thought he had lit a fire under Gene's derriere. Determined to beat us to it, or so he said, he began construction in the dead of winter. He gave Dan the idea to inlay netting under the deck boards. Willa was all smiles and thanked us. She now had a deck and someone who can motivate her husband. He was a master plumber and Stuart was a plumber and a chef. He took care of both ends. Willa was an LPN at Spring Grove Mental Hospital. She bought her clothes from Goodwill and canned a wheelbarrow full of tomatoes. Stuart would hunt deer on the 80 acre West Virginia property that belonged to Willa that he would inherit one day. The WV house was jacked up. It needed work. Stuart would skin the deer right on his deck on a picnic table. His deck was higher than ours and we're right next door, so you get the picture. One time he had baby ducks that grew up to be adult ducks and I gave him our old baby pool. It was fun for my kids to watch them flap around in the water, but it was not fun to smell them. Stuart was too busy to clean up the yard. I begged him to do something, so he did. He got rid of the ducks. Then he had a German Shepherd and he was so proud of him, that day that Duke killed a rat. He called me outside to see it. It just confirmed the thought that we needed to move. I remember cleaning out the sandbox with rubber gloves and my neighbor, Al,the elderly man across the alley,(He and his wife were always watching the children play),yelled over to me to throw all of the toys away, that rats had been in there. The following Sunday when I was nursing my baby Danielle before church, Danny said, "Now don't get excited. There is a rat walking up our pavement in the backyard." How does one not get excited when you have three babies who will play out there? We called the county and a man inspected the yard and around the house. He said there was no evidence of infestation. *Be sure there is never any food in the yard. The alleys are right there and they live under alleys in the sewers, after all.*

One day, I heard a rumbling under the steps that lead to the basement. It went on for days. Of course, whenever

I called someone to come listen, there was no noise. Finally, a week later,Danny heard it. He and *Stu Baby* ripped up a couple of steps and beat that thing to death. It was a rat or else a very large mouse. Stuart said I fed it better than my children. Have I mentioned that I hate rodents? I had stood on a chair in front of my 6th grade class when the gerbil had escaped its cage. And I was the teacher!

I jumped up and down, screaming, when I had looked down at my foot in the laundry room and saw something furry by it. My neighbor Jim came over because Dan was working. He brought a trap but told me it will take a little time because it won't be in the exact same spot. He came back upstairs laughing. *You must have given him a heart attack because he's flat out dead in the same spot.* And then he added, *or else you stepped on him.* I was pregnant too.

Another time, little Timmy asked his father if mice climb walls. He was in the basement bathroom. Danny was in the workshop. You could hear his power saw shrieking.He comes out with a hand made spear in his hands and a gleam in his eye. *Where is he? Where is he, son?* Timmy pointed to the concrete wall, painted bright green, and he couldn't stop laughing. The mouse was scurrying up the wall, even though *mice can't climb.* Danny speared him like some savage from the Zulu tribe.

A few years before at our Cedar Drive house (the cape cod), there was a gargantuan bee (a carpenter bee, what else!) behind the glass of the fireplace doors. My car was in the shop, neighbors were at work, and my babies, Michelle and Anna, were stranded with me. It freaked me out, thinking it will find its way out and sting my girls. I could even see its mouth chewing when I stared it down. So I called my father who told me to call the police. I did. Do you think a cop came over? So I swooped up the girls on that hot humid day and we spent it out on the screened porch.They were miserable, hot and sweaty, wanting to nap in their cribs. I was pregnant of course and exhausted from emotion. But go inside? Too risky.

So how did we solve our problem, the fact that mice felt right at home in our rowhouse? We didn't. In early fall, there appeared a tabby kitten, gray and black with bull's eye markings, (how appropriate), right on our window sill. Every night we sat at out trestle table in the dining room and listened to the kitten's mewing and the children's begging, *Can we keep him?* It started with a little bowl of milk, then a basket and a blanket. He always returned to us each evening. The air was getting frisky and so were the children, so Danny gave in and opened the kitchen door. Immediately, the kitty hid under the bulky antique buffet in the dining room and committed diarrhea. Danny cleaned it up with a sigh. Did I mention that Danny hates cats? Bibs, who had a white area under his chin, adopted us. Since Bibs had become part of our family, not one mouse braved to enter. Bibs was talented. He played a toy piano and found his way out of the toy box Timmy kept stuffing him into. But he scratched baby Kelley near her eye and we had to spend money we did not have to get him declawed and neutered while we were at it. Then Michelle showed signs of allergy and I had to choose. My neighbor, Elaine, found him a loving home in New Windsor in Carroll County. He made it out there before we did! Danielle and I were hysterical with grief. No one else seemed to mind. Until we moved to Carroll County and my neighbors, Pat and John, gave us a single white female kitten to which her daughter was allergic. She had a gray streak on top of her head and they named her Gracie. Alyssa and Kelley begged and cried and hugged their daddy around his neck tightly until he said *yes.* Actually, his exact words were: *All right, I guess.* It was our insurance, after all, that no mouse would dare to enter. We never had a mouse.

But we had snakes. Timmy studied them from library books and the internet. So when one was spotted in the basement in Michelle's bedroom that her father had made for her, Timmy, age 8, just picked it up and took it to the nearby woods. Another was spotted curled up in the hallway. Timmy again knew just how to pick it up. And then Timmy actually brought one into the house and it showed its fangs and hissed at me. That's when I realized Tim loved snakes. We compromised and let him buy two lizards. He was in elementary school and science was his favorite subject. He made a habitat in an aquarium. One day when Dan was riding his mower, Timmy frantically ran into the house shouting that, *he can't hear and he won't stop. I dropped the lizard in the grass. And it's the good one, Mom.* We said a prayer and then he set out to find him. I didn't want his hopes to crash, so I said probably he won't find him, but go ahead and try. Timmy came back inside with tears in his eyes and a smile that looked like the sun had just come out. He held the lizard in his hand. "See Mom," he said. "I told you I'd find him. You need to have more faith." He was all of 8 years old. What can be more stressful than to see your children broken hearted and you know that you cannot fix this one. Michelle had to leave Eldersburg *pronto* that summer and I helped her by traveling with her to Berlin, right outside of Ocean City and signing for her and Sara to rent a small cottage so she could work at the beach. Anna could not get out of bed for days because her heart was crushed. I spoke to her of hope and strength and God having something better for her . . . day after day. Danielle so many times felt frustrated with this or that and I encouraged her to persevere. There is a time to begin something and a time to end it, but not until you have accomplished or learned what was meant for you. Tim's heart was also broken to pieces but with time and encouragement, his heart rejuvenated and his life became an open door to new experiences and possibilities. He made plans to continue his education out of state, as did Alyssa. She made the decision to end a relationship because of the college life ahead of her, but never thought it meant the loss of a long time friend. When she was going into the fifth grade, her best friend Tracy, then starting Middle School, would come to our house asking for Danielle instead of her. I guess it is an unspoken rule that in Middle School, you don't hang out with someone in Elementary School even if you two had been inseparable up to now. Alyssa looked at me with her big dark eyes, teardrops like pearls moistening her cheeks, and her innocence asking, *why.* Kelley was not exempt from heartbreak either, only she could not find reason for it. It was a pervasive feeling of heavy heartedness and loneliness, and I remember so well suffering like that at her age. At 19, you are considered an adult who has his or her life all mapped out, but in reality, most of us do not and the world can then become a frightening and insecure place. I suggested to my children that they keep a journal of their true feelings, attitudes, hopes, frustrations, and dreams. I also told them to stop beating themselves up, that things will change for the better, that life is always changing. "To everything there is a season, a time for every purpose under heaven . . . a time to weep and a time to laugh, a time to mourn and a time to dance." (Ecclesiastes 3:1,4) I prayed they'd dance. You want to say just the right word at the right time and you want to see instant healing . . . but healing takes time and the strength we gain through that painful process is priceless. The heart is broken and each piece has to be mended, day by day. I learned that just by being there for them, the process is already started.

Chapter Six

WAITING ON DANNY

My dad knew how to wait. He waited with patience for my mom to finish her shopping. He took Danielle to each one of her numerous ear operations when she was a child. And he waited and waited with my mom and me. He was quiet and he was always there. When he was waiting for yet another dangerous dye test which seeks out any good arteries left after the ravages of heart disease, he grabbed my hand and neither one of us spoke. When he was in the ICU for the last time, he asked me if I was ever afraid to close my eyes and sleep for fear of never waking up again. Still, he waited silently and then bravely gave up the battle, slapping the bed to resist the pain, and then passing ever so gently into a place of light and peace.

When my daughter Anna had her secret operation of breast augmentation that *the family* was not supposed to know about, I waited in a chair for eight hours, afraid to take a break until I knew everything was okay. A phone in the waiting room would ring to alert someone that it is time to go see your loved one in recovery. Just when my "waiting nerves" were thinning like a worn shoelace about to break, the phone rang for me. Anna was still not clear headed enough to leave, but at least I was out of that seat and *thank God and Dr. Kanter she is fine. Think anyone will notice she has grown from a B cup to a D cup?*

This supreme act of waiting was born out of many raw, rough, rusty, splintery moments of going out of my mind waiting for someone else. That person was Danny.

I was on the front lines, fully armored, shredding to bits every thought that remotely smelled of fear; that is, until the clock read 1 a.m. and still I did not hear a truck pull up. It must have been the angels who awakened Michelle and led her to my side. We waited together. I was clutching baby Kelley and making permanent footprints on the wooden floor. Michelle was quiet, studying me and then deciding to say, "Don't worry, Mom, he'll come home soon." Worry? I was beyond the forest of worry where you cannot see what is happening. I had entered the swamp of *now we are sinking because something bad must have happened or why hasn't he called and my children and I will be orphans together!* The armor I was wearing? Cracked! Michelle ended up pacing with me as if the more mileage we gain going from living room to kitchen and back again would surely bring home her daddy in one piece. Danny had an often dangerous job as a carpenter. He'd be walking steel beams 50 or more feet high, working underground in a subway tunnel, forming up for concrete in bottomless pits, and working late at night in lonely warehouses in the murder districts of Baltimore City, where not only street lamps cast their shadows. He had called at 3:30 that afternoon and said he would be working overtime. He had called again at 9 p.m. and said *a little while longer.* The key wiggled in the lock at 4a.m. Our night vigil had ended. Danny said, "Sorry, Baa, I just couldn't call you. You shouldn't worry. Trust in the Lord." There's that word again: trust. It's only five letters. That night I vowed that I would hide those letters inside my heart. Michelle climbed the stairs for bed, relieved and probably already feeling a little older. It is peculiar how much birth order affects our perspective. At ten years of age, Michelle, my oldest, was already my able teenager on whom I could depend. When my youngest, Kelley, was ten, she was still the one who needed us to do things for her, like, *leave the worrying to us and you go play.* Remember, there were no cell phones in those days, only the battle between blind faith and fear.

That night was not an isolated incident. Only weeks before, when Kelley was only 2 weeks old, Danny was again *missing in action.* Here it was, nearing midnight, and I was beyond exhausted having six children now and little sleep. Danny was part of the vestry *ghostbusters* team, investigating suspicious activity at the church, which eventually put one of the priests in jail for child pornography. Okay. Worthy cause to be late, but he forgot one thing:he didn't call me. So I had no time to prepare myself for such sensibilities as u*nderstanding and reason.* So when he showed up at the back door of our rowhouse, I catapulted over there and locked it. He just kept knocking and laughing. I growled at him. So he just sat down on the deck and waited. Waited in silence, like my father would do. Only I think my father in this circumstance would have yelled something and knit his dark eyebrows together. Danny was amused probably because he was drunk with fatigue himself. He wasn't going to walk around the block to get to the front door, either. When my eyes tired from glaring at him, I unlocked the door. He said it was nice out there, peaceful, watching the bats fly in and out of our neighbor's attic, two doors up. I then turned into superwoman and picked up the kitchen chair and slung it across the floor. I pounded the table with my fist and screamed, in a most unattractive voice, *Why are you so late? You were at church, for God's sake! Why didn't you call?* Danny honestly didn't know what to say. He just hugged me with all the strength he had left and I was struggling to get loose like I had on a straight jacket. Finally, he let go. I cried. We went to bed. At five a.m. the next morning, he bent down and kissed me good bye. I got up soon after and nursed my baby before getting myself ready for the day and waking up the kids for school. We lived too close for bus service but I did not feel comfortable with them walking past apartments to get to school, so I drove. Danny came home as usual, with a smile on his face, loving his family, loving his job, loving life. And I smiled, knowing how much I love him and the children we made together. Life as usual. Last night was just a bad dream.

They say opposites attract. I am a doer and Dan is a *let me think about it for a month or two* kind of guy. We had moved into our brand new home on Holt Court in Carroll County and there were stacks of pictures I wanted hung. Every night I returned from teaching night school at 11p.m. and he'd have my dinner hot in the oven, but no pictures hung. Finally after a couple of months, I threatened to pick up a hammer and nail. He immediately shot up off the sofa, canon-like, and started hanging. Procrastination has two sides to it. One is, I really don't feel like doing it, so it can wait . . . the other is, I will do it when it is no longer a big deal to do it. I hate the second side more. It was a domino effect. The screened in porch that Danny made was our new summer room which we loved, but it made the family room dark and dreary in the winter. So a triple window was in order. Danny thought it was a great idea and said he would do it soon. Soon? What does that mean in procrastination language? By the time he had actually broken through the wall and set up the plastic, I, too, was broken. In spirit, that is. It got to the point, I really did not care anymore. I told him not to do it and we'll just have to live in a dreary house. That argument hissed and growled until three o'clock in the morning. The kids thought we were going to get a divorce, because they could not remember us ever fighting. They key word is *us*. Usually it was just one of us angry and the other one calming him or me down. This time, it was both of us angry at each other. Unheard of in our marriage. This was the one and only time both of us were stoking the fire. When that fire died, we never lit it again. It was too draining and too absurd. We love each other, after all. What was it worth? A triple window?

I blame it all on stress, the underlying midstream that just cuts you in half if you let it. My parents had come over to see the project. They walked smack into our marital spat. Dad said, "Gee, I was hoping you two could cheer me up, today. Guess I was wrong!" Mom said, "I'm embarrassed." What was she embarrassed about? I deserved to be out of control sometime! That's when I added *power walking* around the neighborhood to my daily exercise routine. I highly recommend it.

Chapter Seven

PADDLING AND PUNISHMENT

Each of our children was well behaved in public, whether at church, at school, at the mall, at a restaurant (like McDonald's), or at someone's house. No problems. But human nature being what it is, we all are born anxious to learn that one powerful word that defies all parental authority: the word *no*. It begins at age two and that is when spanking becomes a household word. *Do you want a spanking?* Now, who in his right mind wants a spanking? But Danny and I asked that stupid question again and again, to which little heads would shake in the negative, and sometimes in a "positive" vein, then go ahead and do what they were intending to do in the first place. That's when I would give a little whack, smack on the behind. Then, a quick hug and say *I love you* and then, *How about a cookie?* When they were of the elementary school age, no cookies. Danny, on the other hand, had a whole routine worked out. I used to teach at St. Timothy's Parish School before I had children. There was a fellow teacher who evolved as "The Chief Paddler." I did not feel comfortable spanking another person's child, and over what, really? So after 3 demerits earned, I would send my student to him. My church, St. Timothy's, was a big proponent of using the wooden spoon. "He who spares the rod, hates his child." (Proverbs 13:24). Let me tell you, *A Whole Lotta Love* went into those spankings (Led Zeppelin playing in my head).

Danny's routine went like this: He looks at the offender right in the eyes and says, "Come into the living room." We are in our country home and we have double doors to our living room, which Danny shuts. He then asks, "Do you know what you did wrong?"

The answer to this question, the offender never knows. Danny proceeds to inform. Then he says, "Let's see what The Lord thinks about this." He reads a scripture and then closes the Bible. This is when you hear a whimper or a sniffle. He says, "Bend over." Then, *whack,* no more than 3 of them. Tears, red face, and sometimes anger instead of remorse, nonetheless, Danny then hugs the guilty one, not letting him or her go until he tells the child, "I love you." Sometimes, it is a struggle because the child does not want a hug from a father who just whacked him or her. Danny always ended the session with, "All is forgiven and forgotten."

Forgotten? It depends from whose perspective the spanking came. Spanking, as a family institution, ended at age eight. Dr. James Dobson, a world renowned child psychologist, defined the spanking age as 2 to 8. He was right. At age 8, Michelle just stood there laughing when Danny held a spoon in his hand and had just closed those double doors. He gave up.

There are other ways to discipline when needed, like getting *grounded.* I had only twice ridden in an airplane, myself, and was never grounded, so I really did not understand that concept as well as I should have. My sense of *grounded* was, *okay, you can have a couple of friends over, but you cannot leave the house.* Danny would come home from work with a smiling face, soiled with construction dirt, and then look puzzled because the *grounded one* was laughing with her friends. "Baa, that's not what *grounded* means!" To which I would reply, "She's home, isn't she?"

When the wooden spoon cracked in half on Danielle's bottom, and she cracked up, we resorted to the next logical choice: a ping pong paddle. That worked for a while, but then the paddle mysteriously disappeared. Wouldn't it be stupid if we had asked our children where the paddle is? Well we did. A friend of mine told me his mother used the Tupperware cake taker strap. So I gave it a shot, but my aim was sloppy and I felt bad if it stung their legs. Bad idea. It reminded me of when my dad used to chase us around the dining room table and swipe us with his belt which always braised our legs. We had welts. I certainly did not want that. My cousin's child was bruised by the over zealous grip of her father dragging her to bed. She had refused to leave the computer. At school, she told the teacher her father abused her. The nurse saw a slight bruise and called Social Services. It took two visits from Social Services and a priest's counsel for the state to leave him alone to his parenting. Dan had an idea. He went downstairs to his workshop and all you could hear was the screeching of the power saw. He stomped upstairs holding his prized possession. It looked like a cutting board. We were still in the rowhouse and the children were young. He hung it up on the wall, its thickness casting a shadow. We never had to take it down and actually use it. It was like the speed cameras on the highway. When we moved to the country, somehow the new spanking board was missing. We then picked up the wooden spoon again. Spanking had come full circle.

Telling the truth was the cornerstone of our home. I don't care as much what you did . . . just tell me the truth. Alyssa volunteered all information about another or about herself.

Timmy would just look down at the floor, a dead give away. He knew that if he looked at us eye to eye, he could not hold back the truth. It came tumbling out. Danielle was quiet and just stared at us. Anna told on Michelle and Michelle told on Anna. Kelley was just too cute for us to even imagine she was not telling the truth. Being the "baby" does have its privileges.

I remember calling my dad in desperation. No apartment would take us in because there are eight of us and it is against the fire code in Maryland for so many children to share a three bedroom apartment . . . I even asked for a two bedroom, thinking the living room could have a sleep sofa. No deal anywhere in Catonsville. So Dad told us to pack up our things and live with them. It was only for 4 months while our home in Carroll County was being built. But it was one ice storm after another. The bare trees were heavy laden with fat diamonds, from limb to limb. I had to drive Danielle, Timmy, and Alyssa back to Catonsville, about 30 miles away from Reisterstown, and we arrived at Westowne Elementary late every day. Dan took Michelle and Anna to Diane's house on school mornings. It was 5 o'clock in the morning and they had to hustle to get out the door by 5:30, and the sun wasn't even up yet. They moaned and complained and wore disgruntled faces, while Danny was smiling and urging them to cheer up because this all will be worth it. His mug of coffee wasn't the only thing steaming up those car windows each morning. They attended Catonsville Middle School. Michelle had just been accepted into the *gifted and talented* class because of her portfolio of fashion designs and the cute little figures with the curious expressions who wore them. But the county to which we were moving had no such program. It had farmland, cows, fields of corn, and only one store: K-Mart. Now, Eldersburg is a bit cosmopolitan.

Kelley was three years old and hung out with my father who was retired. He drove my mother to her job at St. Agnes Hospital, quite a hike from where they lived. I had to attend the Community College of Baltimore in Catonsville, taking courses for my certification in teaching, then pick up Alyssa from kindergarten, then bring her to Deer Park Road to Mom and Dad's house, then soon head out again to Catonsville where I taught night school at the local high school. I did not arrive back until 11:30 p.m. Then wake up early and start again. The days I did not teach, I spent hours on course work and lesson plans. So Danny was the sole disciplinarian that winter. All their beds were lined up in the dark paneled basement.

We hung a curtain between the two rooms in which we fit our entire bedroom suite. There was no bathroom down there and only two small windows on the kids' side. It was pitch dark on our side. In the morning when I climbed the stairs and entered the kitchen with light streaming out of the five pane bow window, I was blinded and stumbled down the long hallway to the bathroom. That first week, four of the children had a stomach virus, and I was running up and down the basement steps with basins I needed to empty and then quickly replace. Lysol spray was my staple. All of their clothes were hung up on a metal clothes rack which started sagging until collapsing. Dan put up a wooden bar instead. It sagged but did not break. For some unknown reason, we gave Michelle the large guest room upstairs on the main floor that was across from the bathroom. That full sized bed could have fit Anna as well, but we were bent on each one having her and his own bed. In the new house, Timmy had to share a room with Alyssa and Kelley until he was 12 years old and

Danny had completed two bedrooms and a bathroom in the basement, making our home a 6 bedroom house. Anna and Danielle shared a room for a while. Michelle left home at 20, heading to Salisbury University, so Alyssa and Kelley then each had her own bedroom. We were still into the *bed shuffle*, but this time, moving up and down the steps, from the second floor to the basement and back again, was done with the help of boyfriends and Tim . . . .

So the beds had been at my parents' home in the dark basement all lined up in a row like in the orphanage in *Madeline*. I'd come home from night school to hear my brother Anthony retelling the evening's events and laughing so much it grew contagious. Apparently, this was a regular evening routine. Dan would notice that they hadn't made their beds or straightened up the basement. He lined them all up and spanked with the spoon, ages 8 and under, all four. Anthony sat on the step and laughed until tears. He said he wouldn't miss it for the world. *The best entertainment!* Apparently, one night while Danny was washing the dishes, suds everywhere, Danielle was standing at his elbow and insisting he stop and sign a paper she needed for school. He said he would do it later, to which little Danielle replied, *Sign it BuddyBoy.* Can you imagine an 8 year old looking up at her father who is 6 ft.2? To whom was she speaking? For one thing, he's her father. Another thing, he is a procrastinator. Fat chance he would make any effort to sign it while she was still awake that night. I am sure she cried from frustration. Danny probably did too!

I was soon growing weary from strict punishments. *You're grounded for two weeks* turned into one week. *I'm pulling your car keys for two weeks* turned into three days. Then I had become the chauffeur, as well as a substitute teacher, housekeeper, arbitrator, counselor, chef, and laundry maid. I still cannot forgive myself for sprinkling pepper on Danielle's tongue and not allowing her to sleep over at Kristen's birthday party, because it was reported that she had said a dirty word to my brother, one of a sexual nature. I should have asked her where she had heard that word and told her not to use it again, let alone to a grown man. Instead, I had become enraged. Danny and I did not cuss and expected our children to do the same. One time I said the f word behind closed doors. I don't remember why, but I remember that the next day, Anna told me she heard me, and to this day she says, *Mom, you say the f word.* And it's been 14 years since I did. Years ago, I heard Alyssa say to one of her friends, *My mom cusses!* as if it's a cool thing to do. With children, *one time* and you are hung for life! Probably because I would always remind them that it is what comes out of the mouth that makes you dirty and not what goes in. That's from the Bible and that's before I became health conscious enough to switch to 100% whole wheat bread, yogurt, bran cereal, fresh fruit, and Smart Balance. In those days we were stocked with Little Debbie's and canned soda (generic of course). Probably the healthiest food we did eat was pizza, every Friday night in the rowhouse. We watched *Full House, Perfect Strangers, Family Matters, Bill Cosby* and *One Step At A Time* Friday nights. On Saturday nights, we had board games. We must have owned over 30 of them. I can remember taking the game "Operation" back to the store because the buzzer noise scared them. It goes that far back. Needless to say, when we were having fun as a family, all of the stressful, tense moments of spanking and punishing were tucked away and maybe never even happened at all. What wooden spoon?

In our country house, we have an old fashioned trap door in the basement, leading out of Dan's workshop. More than once we heard the slam of those metal doors and raced to the front door just in time to see a getaway car speeding up the street with *grounded* Timmy in the passenger seat. Of course, it was late at night and we were supposed to be sleeping as all good parents should be. And there was Anna who was grounded but begged to stay at Nonna's for a few days because she had to get away. Just like when she begged to get stranded at Nonna and Pop-Pop's during a full blown snow blizzard. She was at home with us. We trudged through the snow in our Caravan, dropped her off, then headed right back, with my father looking at us incredulously. I think we did it for my parents more than we did it for Anna. It's their adorable granddaughter after all. We had more at home where that came from. Staying at Nonna's can never be a punishment and Anna knew it.

So for what does a parent spank or punish? Timmy messing up Michelle's Barbie dolls and Barbie clothes? Something not nice said on the bus and later denied? Picking flowers from someone else's garden? Not picking up your toys? Hitting a brother or sister? And how does this compare to inviting 200 people to your house because your parents are vacationing at Ocean City (with Alyssa and Kelley, the only ones who would still go with them)? How about coming home to a neighbor, who happens to be a policewoman, saying that she sat on her porch and counted the cars and they were lined all the way up the hill. But funny thing, shades were drawn and no loud music could be heard. If my children could have hidden the cars, they would have. The only bad report was a sack of flour dumped on a neighbor's car by someone who was refused entrance to *the party of the year*. Reportedly, police would visit and then leave and the party would go on. This became a *rite of passage*, a yearly tradition until it was Kelley's turn and

Timmy, being older now and more mature, kicked everybody out and then called to tell us so. After thanking him, Kelley called us and said it was *not fair*, a classic complaint coming from every teenager that was ever born. I told her I was sorry. I did not know what to say because she was right. From her perspective, it *was* not fair! She is a Cook. It is her tradition also, maybe even her right. There I go again, thinking about what is fair and not fair and it is all so confusing. Anyway, the parties ended. They evolved to just "get together." *Mom, can I have a get together tonight? Just a couple of people.*

There were actually behaviors that went unpunished because I had every confidence that my children could handle the situation on their own. Michelle just walked up to Anna in the high school cafeteria at Liberty High and demanded she take off the shirt she had taken from her. Anna took it off right there, having worn another shirt underneath just in case. Another time, Michelle could not find her favorite dress. Anna had no clue. She solicited my help. I searched until I found it, balled up in the corner under Anna's bed, though she swore she did not take it. This went on for years until the girls treated their bedrooms like apartments and locked up before they left. Guess who also locked her room? Anna.

When they were little, I would ask, "Whose team do you want to be on? God's or the devil's?" They knew all about God and the devil through countless Sunday School classes and countless summers of Vacation Bible School, as well as our very own Bible Study at home. When it got to the years that only Alyssa and Kelley were now present for our family Bible sessions, it always ended up in Dan and I getting angry and someone getting punished. We were frustrated. What was the point? Alyssa would roll her eyes and then start to giggle. Kelley would follow suit, so willing to walk down that road with her sister every time. Alyssa then took it to another level and would hold her ears and sing *Lalalalala* right as I was teaching God's word. That's when Dan and I realized our family Bible time was over, just like our Family Meetings were also over. No one was available at the same time any longer, with work schedules, school activities, and a full social calendar. I started leaving notes on the refrigerator door in black magic marker. I started copying scripture and posting it on the refrigerator. No more dish schedules were hanging up. And we no longer sat down at the dinner table together. It seems that after-school-jobs had torn our family time apart. We taught our children to become resourceful and earn their own money to get the things they needed, and in some cases, wanted. It was a necessary sacrifice, and though communication was not the same, and nor was the dinner table, I could always count on my children to open the refrigerator door.

CHAPTER EIGHT

A PARENT'S WISDOM

Proverbs, a book in the Bible written by wise King Solomon, chapter one describes wisdom as a woman who calls out to people in the concourses of the town to listen to what she has to say. She yells, "How long will you cling to stupidity?" This tells me that wisdom has a voice that we will never hear, *mai e poi mai*, if we are too busy listening to ourselves. Wisdom comes from God who created the world through it. So how do I listen?

Danny watches the news like some people raid the refrigerator, gobbling up everything in sight. The 5pm news is the appetizer. The 6pm news is the meal. The 7 pm news is the dessert. (world news). The 10 pm news is the "midnight snack". He rarely skips a meal. Back in the day when the kids were small, he watched the early news and then waited until 11pm to watch more news. I caught some of it as I flew up and down the basement steps. Michelle, with her deep set, dark, contemplative eyes, also watched the news while she played. That must be the explanation for the paranoia that slithered into her soul. Whenever we were at the mall, Michelle's eyes would turn panic-stricken. "Mommy, we *have* to go. Tell Daddy to hurry up. We're gonna get shot! C'mon.! Go! Now!" It was like snake poison. She was pallid and we had to leave immediately. When I said, "Everything is all right", still she didn't believe me. Danny started skipping the evening news in hopes that those images of guns and criminals would go to the recycle bin in her brain until she was old enough to realize the danger but not become crippled by it. Michelle would not spend the night at her best friend Lindsay's house during that time. She'd call me to pick her up because she thought something bad was going to happen. But no news is good news. Eventually, that whole paranoia thing left her in peace. Wisdom was calling and we were finally listening, *that time*!

Another time, Michelle was told not to run on the gravelly church parking lot. Of course she ran, like any young child would do. She fell down into the stones, as any young child would do. At home, Danny suddenly decided he was a doctor. He cleaned it well and then poured hydrogen peroxide on it as double protection. He applied gauze and tape and it looked like she had just come from the Emergency. Well done, except for that little itsy bitsy comment I had made, that I thought I saw a white thing inside the lesion. Is it a stone or bone? Danny replied, "It's nothing. Just your imagination. What you saw is just the blood clotting." Wisdom was calling but who was listening? I accepted his answer. A few months later, it was becoming increasingly more difficult for Michelle to kneel, like in gym and when in prayer with us at home. You could not blame it on the healing process any longer. It was healed all right! There was a bump inside the center of her knee. And it was pointy, no less, and embarrassing. Now *that* was a kick in the ass. Was Dr. Dan remorseful? "Well, why didn't you insist we take her to the hospital? You do at other times!" I don't know why. I guess I trusted that *maybe this time* his instincts were keener than mine. What's wrong with me? I and every other woman on this planet knows that only women are born with these kinds of instincts when it comes to taking care of children. Men have to acquire them. We found a surgeon and Michelle was operated on promptly. Dr. Middleton showed us the stone. I should have saved it as a sharp reminder that one should always listen to her (or his) inner voice. Why cling to stupidity?

I remember a time when Danny was nurse to us all. He was running the marathon of meeting everyone's needs every day he returned home from work. It went on for days, babies in diapers and Timmy, Michelle, and I flat on our backs, sick with the flu. Michelle was on the top bunk in the "dormitory" in our rowhouse. I was at the boiling point with fever and tried to yell for ice chips, but my voice was probably one octave higher than the squeak of a mouse. But something besides a sere throat was getting my attention. Was it a feeling or did I actually hear my thoughts spoken out loud? My mind was fuzzy but something inside me was clear and decisive. My legs felt like skinny reeds fighting a windstorm, and I put two unsteady feet on the wooden floor. Still, something inside me was propelling me on. When I entered Michelle's room, she sat up in her top bunk bed and asked me to get her a drink from the water fountain in the hall. Just one look at her, let alone what she said, told me that we cannot call Dr. Young soon enough. Funny that she talked about the water fountain. When I was a little girl and delirious with fever, I asked my mother the exact same thing in the Greenlow Road rowhouse down the street in the same Academy Heights. It was midnight when I called Dr. Young in answer to Dan's comment, "At this hour?!" Like I said, it is an acquired instinct that men need to cultivate when they become fathers. I have to say that in the midst of all this cultivating, Danny gave his heart to our children 24-7. Without hesitation, he swept up spindly Michelle in his strong arms and saved her without a cape. He spent the next three days and nights with her in the hospital. At five a.m., just as I predicted, on a Wednesday morning, Michelle called me crying that her daddy was gone. I full well knew that he had to return to work or we would not eat. While on the phone, I heard some nurse scold my daughter and accuse her of being a *cry baby.* I wanted Michelle to put her on the phone. The nurse told me she was disturbing the floor with her "carrying ons." I told her that Michelle is frightened and that it is up to the nurses to make her feel safe. I also told her I am coming in. My dad took me for moral support. As soon as we walked in, I smelled something nasty. I resisted becoming nasty, but could not get to the desk soon enough to tell a nurse to change Michelle's bed linens and why was my daughter in this situation in the first place? It was clear to me that my daughter was being ignored because someone had judged her to be too old to be crying for daddy on a pediatric floor. I was livid but controlled. I reported it to Dr.Marston Young who became livid. He always treated my children like precious jewels. He had words with the nurses at the hospital.

He also discharged Michelle, telling me at this point she will get much better care at home so there is no longer any cause to upset her. Michelle recovered from Scarlet Fever without any residual effects. Not to say the hospital did not have any! When my mother was a little girl, she too had Scarlet Fever. But in the early 1920's, things were done differently. Her bedroom became a sterile hospital room and everything that could be burned in a bonfire, was burned upon her recovery. My grandmother, Palsie, believed that it left Anna, my mother, *nervous.* So we were left to believe that Mom could not control her *nervousness.* It's not her fault she got Scarlet Fever! We just had to suffer silently because of it. Well thank God, Michelle did not get that because it is a lifelong condition.

Michelle was strong willed and determined as a child, and a teenager, and is true to form as a young woman. When she was but five and wore that "hideous" cast on her leg, I recall Palsie (Rose) and her sister, Aunt Anna, coming over to see Michelle Rose for a little visit. Michelle stood in the kitchen on crutches, her long brown hair touching her waist, her very brown eyes deep set in thought, her eyebrows knit, and her posture slightly bent. She looked up at me and said matter of fact, "Make them go home!" Palsie heard it and said, "Michelle, honey, don't say that. We want to see you." But it had been said and Michelle was not one to dishonor her own word. at the tender age of five. So be it. Palsie Rose and Aunt Anna went home. Should I have made her see them? Was this a power struggle? I saw it as a little girl who positively hated the fact that she broke her leg and her world is altered. She did not want anyone doting on her condition and reminding her that *soon it will all be better.* "Soon" means absolutely nothing to the one who wakes up in the same condition every day and has to cope with it minute by minute. So how many minutes are in a day? Did I mention it feels like a lifetime? Embarrassed? Yes, I was. Understanding? Yup.

I was convinced that Michelle had no residual effects from Scarlet Fever until she grabbed me in panic and asked me to look at her skin. Her arms were blue, the color of veins through transparent skin, like on old people. Her upper back and chest also. I felt her panic invade my blood and I felt twinges of fear sprinting through my veins. Is this a sign of *leukemia?* I pressed the buttons of the phone at record speed. "Hello, Doctor? Something is wrong with Michelle!" We now visited another practice because our revered Doctor Young had to retire from his for health reasons. A female doctor answered my call with the mind set of a mother, herself. After I answered her many questions, she started laughing. She had a hunch that the blueness was from the dye on her new shirt, and that I should wash the shirt as well as her skin, and then call her back. She was right and I was feeling rather foolish. I always thought of myself as level headed, that is, until I became a mother. So Michelle had become a little overly concerned about her health. I was sure it would pass as she grew up and realized that most of the time we worry about things that will never ever happen, *mai e poi mai*.

Then there are those times when our worst fears do come true and then what do we do? It was Michelle's 16th birthday and she was determined to get her driver's license that very day. She was to be our first driver. My car was the *famous foul smelling white Oldsmobile* that my father had so graciously given me. When Michelle and Anna were younger, they were passengers in the back seat, my mother driving furiously and fearlessly down the road on the way home from Security Square Mall in Catonsville where she had indulged them each with a new wardrobe. She was always shopping with her grandchildren, which included bags of groceries as well as clothing and shoes. Coming home from this one trip forever changed the fate of her beloved Olds. It was winter but the sun was branding the car windows with heat. The girls were bundled up with scarves, hats, and mittens as well as buttoned up coats. Nonna turned up the heat because it was as cold as Iceland outside. Too bad, in the back seat it was Tahiti! Then the fateful words: "Nonna, I think I am going to throw up," says Anna. "No you're not!" my mother commands. "But if you do, use your hat." Where was that woman named Wisdom calling out in the concourses? Was she on a lunch break? We all know that little knit winter caps are just that, they are knit. As soon as Anna vomited and it seeped right through the cap and onto the floor, so did Michelle into her knit cap, upon my mother's orders. Mom pulled up to our house and before she finished yelling, *I need your help*, I was out there with my scrub bucket of scalding hot water, Mr. Clean, and lots of rags. My dad had the car professionally cleaned after he spent hours washing the entire interior trying to tame that smell. No chance. It growled and clawed and just tore up your sense of smell until you felt like you were going to get sick. The curse of the car! So naturally, I inherited that car since Michelle and Anna had branded it for me. Thanks! I did not have a car at the time and desperate times create desperate people. This is the very car Michelle took to Westminster to get her license on her birthday September 4th. It was hot that day and it was my guess that the policeman who sat beside her would hurry the test just to get the hell out of that car. True to the curse, it reeked of vomit. It was the smell of an evil spirit that haunted the car I refused to call mine. It refused to leave. And just to be spiteful, as all sprites are, it started to emit smoke from the hood like a Medieval dragon just as Michelle was finishing her driving test. "Out," the cop said. "The test is over." To whom did he think he was speaking? This is a child who defied her great grandmother at the age of five. This is a child who had Smurf skin and panicked me to call the doctor. She asked the cop who was big bellied, middle aged, and stern, if she could still take the test today if she can get another car. He said yes. "Mom, you've got to ask somebody." The somebody I thought of is Janine, my sweet neighbor who has children of her own the ages of my Timmy and Kelley, then 8 and 4. She had just trudged into her house carrying bags of groceries when she answered the phone. "Sure, Barb. As soon as I put away my groceries." We were 30 miles away. Michelle got behind the wheel of Janine's little sedan and drove it with confidence and ease, as if it were her own car. She smiled for her first license photo. This was the little girl who would not give up her diapers until *she* decided. This was the little girl who wet the bed every night until faced with the possibility of taking medicine, and *on the spot* decided she would not wet anymore, even though the wetting was an unconscious act. Of course she got her license on the day of her birthday, smoking car or not. *She decided*!

Back to the car . . . Should I have accepted that car? Being that my Dad was the gifter, I would have had to strain to hear Wisdom because she would have been whispering. I didn't. Then there's the relationship between father and son where wisdom is a constant companion because fathers live and breathe it. Am I right? There is a right way to cast off a fishing line and there is a wrong way. Tightly wind up the reel, release the lever and then sling it out like you are throwing a football for a touchdown. Once it touches down in the water, engage the lever so it locks. When a fish tugs, jerk the line so that its lip gets hooked. Gotcha! If you have an interesting lure on the end of your line, you might catch an interesting fish. Just like if you tell your son exactly how to throw out his arm for distance, and how to sling the line to the side with a flick of his wrist like when playing ping-pong, he'll get it right every time, bushes or no bushes. The first time Dan took Timmy, 8, out to the Liberty Reservoir to teach him to fish, lesson one was, *casting off.* He decided to show rather than tell, step by step : *wind up*, r*elease, sling arm to the side, flick wrist, ping-pong, avoid the bushes, sling, sling, watch me . . . Are you watching? This is nuts! I can't believe it.* The line is now tangled up in the bushes, Timmy is laughing, and Danny is shaking his head.

And how did I know about this little lesson? Timmy told me as soon as he got home. *Mom, guess what?*

Besides always tell the truth, the best advice he gave to Timmy in his early years was concerning a bully in the first grade. Timmy was twice his size and gentle in spirit. Yet this kid would kick him in the back or rear end every day at dismissal when Tim bent over to get his things from the "cloak room" to take home and the teacher wasn't looking. We told him to report it to the teacher and every day it was the same: "I did not see him, Timmy. Sorry. "It was getting to the point that I wanted to walk into that classroom and push the teacher and say, "Sorry. The principal isn't looking." Dan then took Tim aside after dinner one evening and said, "I am sorry it has to come to this but sometimes there is a kid who will not respect you until you put him in his place. This kid is that kind of kid. So when the teacher isn't looking, and before you get your things, take your two hands and push that kid into the closet with everything you got!" Tim did. From then on, he hung around Tim and tried to win his friendship. He never did. Lesson learned. Respect earned. During the middle school years when Tim hung out with the neighborhood boys in Eldersburg Estates, our new residence, things were not always cool, like the time they were all playing basketball and just when Tim was going for a basket, his friend purposely puts out his foot and trips him. Blood everywhere. Tim couldn't play anymore. Of course, the adults thought it was an accident. Tim knew better but did not say anything. He was a meek little boy and unfortunately, kids mistake this for weakness, as do some adults. Meekness is a controlled strength. Like father like son.

Dan always said talk it out and then let it go. But what if the other kid will not let go of you? On the bus, this same kid started to call Timmy "a girl." Tim talked to him.

Tim talked to the kid's father. Nothing changed. He came home one day extremely agitated and said, "Mom, I can't take it anymore. I can't hold back. I'm going to hit him." I say, "Okay, do it here in the street after school. I'll be watching. Tell him it's a show down" Timmy was swinging and the kid was sprinting, weaving in and out to avoid the hit, literally running circles around him. The father runs up and says, "Whoa, guys. What's going on?" I yell out my kitchen door, "It's okay. We'll both watch and let them settle their differences. Nothing else has worked." "Okay", the father says. Timmy finally got one punch in, right in the face, and the kid immediately turned and ran like hell back home. Things were settled. No more teasing. They remained friends. In fact, the boy's parents are friends of ours to this day. And the mother of this boy? She's the sweet woman who drove up to Westminster so that Michelle could get her license. Whoever expects their children to be perfect is missing the mark. Were your parents perfect? Were you a perfect child? Are you now a perfect parent? And who wants perfect, anyway? A little fist fight never hurt anybody, at least maybe only for a little while. Are parents to be blamed for their children's behavior? Not as long as we all have that God given right of free will. Will there be consequences? Just like what Anna said once regarding a party she threw while we were away, "I know I'm punished the rest of the summer, but it was all worth it! My friends will be talking about this party for years. It was the party of the century!" Party on!

Sometimes parents have to make unpopular decisions like, no, you cannot go to Camp Hashawa with your whole class, Danielle, because we just moved here to Carroll County and I don't know these people. They could be perverts. No, children, you cannot go on any field trip that involves walking the Baltimore streets. The zoo? Definitely not. Only if I can go with you. The Science Center at The Harbor? Are you kidding me? My children all knew that a field trip without me meant a day off to stay home and do whatever they felt like doing. The principal would always call and threaten that it is still a school day and it will be considered unexcused. I thought it was inexcusable for teachers to schedule outings in Baltimore City, which was rivaling for the title of *Murder Capital of the Nation, and coming in at second place*. I'd rather have peace of mind and keep my children with me. And this was coming from the principal of a school that did not lock its doors. More on that later.

Wisdom? Do we always hear her calling? Danielle says she so regretted not having the Hashawa experience. All week in school in another classroom was not fun. Timmy, Alyssa, and Kelley were allowed to go, years later. They said they had a blast. You know, to be honest, sometimes you think it's wisdom but it's just plain old fear in disguise. Forgive me, kids. I figured out through the years that if I insisted on my children being in a group chaperoned by someone I trusted, then sure, they could go. I still prayed those six hours while they were gone, but hey, what are mothers for?

CHAPTER NINE

TENT TRAUMAS

It is named Treasure Beach. It is neither a beach nor a treasure. We arrived with our van loaded with our children and a tent. We see a fenced yard with trees and this is of course where you pitch your tent. The spots along the canal where you can enjoy the water and do some fishing? They are reserved for RV's. There is an electrical hook up for them but not for the true campers, the tent people. I guess they figure we are mountain people or gypsies or simply tent dwellers . . . and we don't need electricity for a hair dryer or a little electric camper's stove or a light! So we brought a fry pan and a pot besides our bikinis, swimsuits, and sun screen. Our tent was pitched by Dan only. We assisted under his instruction, *each take a corner and lift.* Not only did we not have a roof over our heads, but we had to create our own! Michelle and Anna were in middle school by now, preteens, and they wore scowls any time the tent was within view, let alone having to be inside it. We actually lit a campfire, cooked scrambled eggs in the pan, and asked Anna and Michelle to bring the little tub of dirty dishwater to the area of disposal. With the look of dread, they were carrying the basin together as if they were disposing of a dead animal. Our tent was red and gray with a little "porch" in the front, actually just a little overhang that fit two chairs. Windows zipped up to screen off the bugs. It had two rooms for eight people. To the younger children, it was fun. To our preteens, it was an embarrassment. To Dan and me, it was an affordable way to spend time at Ocean City.

Our first night ever, we made another campfire and cooked hot dogs. Our neighbors, a couple from Portugal, invited us over to their campsite to roast marshmallows. They spoke English with strong Portuguese accents. Camping across America was their goal. Our goal was to make it through the night. During the day, we headed for the beach. It is only about 4 miles up the road past Harpoon Hannah's Restaurant which sits on the canal and you can watch boats go by while you stuff your mouth with the blueberry, apple, and coconut muffins offered by the muffin girls who carry huge baskets in their arms. We drive over the bridge and soon we are at Coastal Highway, crossing over the line from Delaware into Maryland. The beach is crowded with sunbathers, kids running around, and seagulls swooping low on the crest of white capped waves. Lifeguards signal each other by flapping their flags, boats miles away skidding the water, a person parasailing, a helicopter with an ad banner sailing behind, people swimming, and some standing and holding hands as waves smack their legs, dolphins jumping in and out of the ocean, and pigeons pecking at the sand. The sign at each dune reads: *Leave Nothing But Your Footprints,* but there is always a plastic cup or bottle or two half buried in the sand underfoot as you walk to get to the trash can. We find a spot that is near the water but not too near, considering high tide in the late afternoon will wash away our beach towels and chairs, which we know by experience. Also, what about Sea Nettles and Jelly Fish that wash up on shore? Can sharks do that? We set up. Grease up. Run up. Jump in. Fight waves. Drag sand. Burn our noses. Did I say, "we"? I got wet, ran back to my sand chair wedged in the moist sand, and assisted the lifeguard in watching my children.

Kelley was never afraid of the water. That stage when a child turns two and everything turns scary? Never turned for Kelley. As a toddler, she would run right to the immense ocean as soon as she saw it, just like her older sister Alyssa. Fearless. They still are. In fact all of my children are. The only one who might be reticent to try new things is Danielle, but she is in transformation. Timmy is naturally hungry for adventure, like Alyssa and Michelle. Kelley and Anna are somewhere in between. Danny is brave and I am brave knowing Danny is brave. It rubs off.

My mother used to order McDonald's food for my brother, Anthony, when he was 12 because he thought the name of the burger was silly and he was too embarrassed to say it. You say: *Two all beef patties special sauce cheese and pickle on a sesame seed bun*, or something like that. And because when I needed a mouthpiece, I elected my mother's, I decided to teach my children to speak up for themselves at an early age. *Tell him what you want. Tell her why you think so. Tell me how you feel. You make the phone call. You take this back to the store. You decide.* So crucial. The ocean should be respected but never feared. Same goes for people. So why was I life guarding from a sand chair? A few years earlier, before out tent saga, which lasted all of 6 years, minus Michelle and Anna, (one summer did them in), we rented a large condo, ocean front with big picture windows that made the sky and sea part of the family room's decor. Danny says that we did things *bass-ackwards*. After spending two summers in a condo with a bed to sleep in, a refrigerator to open, and a balcony in which to catch the ocean breezes, who *would* be happy with a tent that is hot as hell inside, where you never really feel clean, and there is no mirror to see what the sweat is really doing to your face, and you are just entering the teenage years and really care about how you look to the opposite sex? The younger children thought it cool to each possess a flashlight and beam it all hours of the night, especially when we had to trek down to the bathhouse in the middle of the night. Back to my question about the sand chair . . . . One summer during the condo years I lost my perspective and thought the beach was my personal day spa. I set myself up in my chair with a drink in one hand and a novel in another. I wore shades, a bikini, an adorable straw hat that looked like a baseball cap, and I smelled like a coconut. All set. What I did not count on was little Danielle getting caught in an undertow right at the edge of the water. Danny, with zinc oxide on his nose, a baggy white tee shirt, and a towel and baby Kelley slung over his shoulder, swooped down into the waves with one arm and saved Danielle. What am I doing? Turning the pages, and thinking, *This is sooo relaxing.* When you are at the spa, you are literally clueless as to what the rest of the world is doing. Hence, the *sand chair patrol* was born. I was insane. My life was not my own. What possessed me to think it was?

After getting all toasted and sugary with sand like a dozen doughnuts, we all headed back to our front yard on Highway 54 at Treasure Beach. It's funny how the littlest most basic things are like heaven or *manna in the wilderness* or *streams in the desert* when camping. I don't know what the bath house for men looked like but I bet you it was cleaner than the women's Maybe it's my upbringing or maybe I have higher standards for bathroom cleanliness than most campers, but I and my girls could not help but scrunch up our faces and then race to the finish line so we could walk out that door. Have you ever taken a shower without getting naked? It's an art. We girls were running a shower marathon. Kelley and I entered the murky waters of a clogged drain. I was ankle deep. Kelley was calf deep. Did we have another option? Well, there was always the pool on the campground. But what about those that pee in it? We were between a rock and a hard place. Did I tell you the shower spray was on a timer? The whole experience sped up your heart rate which can be a good thing. Each evening we broke our record from the previous day. In a flash, we were at the sink as soon as one was available. You learn fast that he who hesitates is lost. It's like crossing the streets of New York on foot. What flashing yellow light of caution? What flashing red light that says *DO NOT WALK*?

You are part of a herd of people who *ain't* stopping. *This* herd consisted of women with unruly long hair that they blow dried like a hurricane and then walked away leaving behind in the sink enough strands to make a wig. And we had to brush our teeth. Whoever watched us probably thought we had electric toothbrushes. I was beginning to think that there are human beings, and then there are campers. This is why one cannot make a judgment based on only one experience. What about 108 experiences? I added up six days a week times six years times three times a day. Could be more. In the early morning when I thought I would beat those wild haired women to the sink, I would be just one of many *refugees* in a long snake of a line waiting for the cleaning lady to exit so we could go in. With my toothbrush in hand and my morning mouth, I began to identify with prisoners of war. How could it get worse? One year we had to camp a quarter of a mile from the bathhouse. I remember power walking to the bathhouse with tears streaming down my face and talking out loud to myself. *What's wrong with that man? Why didn't he call first? I can't put up with this much longer.* We had just arrived and were informed that the yard was closed to campers due to the crafts show. We had to pitch tent alongside the privacy fence, in fact smack against it. What was on the other side? Highway 54 of course. And what did I hear all night long because I couldn't sleep for worry? Eighteen wheelers and speed car racers. What did I see? Headlines: *Whole family* . . . .

That was tornado weekend. Michelle and Anna were home alone in Maryland We were in Delaware with high winds. Three times Danny pitched the tent that weekend. Tent down again! *"For cryin out loud"* he kept exclaiming. I'd already done that, with other campers looking quizzically at me. We happened to grab hold of a newspaper the next morning and couldn't believe what we were reading. A tornado had touched down in Carroll County. Knowing that our house was constructed without plywood, just styrofoam and sticks,(sounds like The Three Pigs), we feared for our girls, hoping beyond hope that they hadn't landed in Oz We found out our good neighbor Rita, one in whose house I could just walk right into and she would offer me a cup of coffee and the time of the day, had alerted them and offered her house so they wouldn't be alone and they could all huddle in the basement together. Instead, they called my father to pick them up and they got the heck out of town. It touched down in Gamber which is about 5 miles from Eldersburg. I was sorry for those people but so thankful to God just the same. The next day, things were looking up. The crafts show was over and we pitched camp inside the yard. It was moved back from Highway 54, but still, an aluminum fence was no match for a big rig. I refused to think about it. It's funny how all things are relative. I was actually smiling again as Danny hammered the stakes into the ground for the third time that weekend. And we were now closer to the bathhouse I abhorred! I was almost giddy with delight!

I can remember only two big mistakes during the tent years. One was buying the tent.

The other was camping at the Delaware Seashore Park. It was on a parking lot, no trees, but the inlet was real close. Danny and the kids fished right there only a few feet from the tent. We had but a short walk to get to the ocean. You know what they say, when it sounds too good to be true, it probably isn't. We could not sleep a wink. The kids had their Rainbow Bright sleeping bags and Timmy had his superhero one, and we slept on a quilt on top of the cement, but we could not shut out the incessant high pitched crying of somebody's infant on one side and the raucous laughter of the men on the other side of us who were drinking all night long. We even asked the man on night shift to speak to them, but they ignored him. The posted rules said *No Noise After 11*.

It was after 2 a.m. and they were just getting started. I guess an unwritten rule is, *Don't mess with drunk campers.* We packed up at the crack of dawn and went home. Dan was so disgusted that he refused to take us to our beloved Treasure Beach instead.

The next summer at Treasure Beach was our last. We were invited to hang out on the beach with some of my cousins and their families, and a few aunts and my own parents. That was the weekend of 10,000 complaints. At this point, just watching Frank Zappa's flick from the 70's, *Two Hundred Motels* would have made them feel better. They felt like they were living a nightmare of 10,000 tents. I remember asking little Alyssa if she needed to go to the bathroom when we arrived at the condo. *Nope.* As soon as we trudged in the sand, carrying all of our junk, as we campers are used to doing, and we sit down with family all around, Alyssa whines that she has to go to the bathroom. I reacted just like any camping mother would. I dragged her across the sands. She fell down and with one arm I yanked her to her feet. I did not know I was the center of my family's attention. My cousin Lisa had remarked, "I think Barbara has had enough." I did not care what they thought. They slept on beds. I slept on a blanket on the hard ground. No one better say a word to me! Why were my nerves like a tattered rope? The whole car ride down to the beach, the kids were cackling about how much they hate camping and why can't we stay in the condo like we used to do? Alyssa and Kelley did not even remember that condo, but they claimed Danielle and Timmy's memory for their own. Complaining is contagious and so is anger. By the time we left that beach, in the van, Danny was yelling that we will never do this again. In fact, he was going to burn the tent. You see, this was the best we could have done those six years. The kids just no longer appreciated our efforts to give them the sand and the ocean each summer. There were summers of body surfing and bogey boarding, and shopping for trinkets and tees on the boardwalk, and rides at the amusement park at Trimper's and The Pier in Ocean City, and eating in restaurants. They forgot all of that and dwelled on the part of coming home each day to a tent. Yeah, we wake up each morning all moist and sticky from the overnight dew, but we ate out and used their restroom, and soon ocean breezes and the surf made us smile again. Let's face it, we Cooks were imposters. Campers, we are not, but we gave it our best shot.

The years that followed, we rented a condo on Ocean Block at our Ocean City, Maryland with an ocean view from the side balcony. Danielle and Timmy were our young teens and each had an adventure. Danielle kept waving to the two boys across the street and pretty soon they met. They asked us if they three could hang out that night and go Put-Put.

Put-Put Golf was one of the highlights of our vacation days those couple of years. We said yes, being impressed that they had extended a hand and asked. After she left, in the days when there were no cell phones, I berated myself, thinking I had suffered a temporary lapse of insanity. Thank the Lord, she came home smiling. Timmy and Danny went out early the next morning to fish in a boat in the ocean. Timmy proudly brought home a filet of Flounder he had caught himself. I pan fried it in Olive Oil for dinner. It gave me a sense of peace, a harmony with nature and my fellow man, I cannot explain it. It was pure, white, and tender and my kids actually liked it. In fact, they liked the entire vacation. Of course, Michelle and Anna no longer vacationed with us. Too sophisticated.

After the years of Ocean Block, we started vacationing with our good friends Sheri and Dave who own a beach house in Bethany Beach, Delaware, one mile from the ocean. At this time, only Alyssa and Kelley wanted to come. Then, it was just Kelley. Then, it was just us. Our children decided they had much better offers vacationing with their friends' families who went to Florida beaches, Disney World, and Myrtle Beach, South Carolina. Friends became more important than family, and Dan and I just had to accept that. It was during our Bethany Beach days that we would get phone calls from Anna Maria who warned us of an upcoming house party, but informed us that she would not be home because she would get into trouble, being over 21 years of age. *Thanks, Anna.* One time we had my brother-in-law, John, check it out and he confiscated all of the beer. No matter. Timmy just went out and got someone to buy him more. You think you are going to outsmart a teenager when you are out of town? Think again. To this day, I cannot get that image of the bathtub full of ice and liquor out of my mind, not to mention the sons and daughters of people I did not know, racing up and down our steps. One time, I found an unopened can of beer in my underwear drawer. I understand it was planted there as a joke. Did they see Dan or me laughing? Wasn't that a clue? Nope. We had more years ahead coming home to red specks splattered on our white kitchen cabinets, traces of vomit in the powder room, one or two beer cans on the lawn, and our children denying that a party ever happened. Remember, *In this house we tell the truth!*

Chapter Ten

THE ALLEY

What was it about the alley that always put dread into my heart? Was it because the cement was broken up and pebbly in places? Was it because cars were parked beside fences and that made a narrow alley even narrower? Was it because I knew those rodents from hell dwelled beneath it? Or was it the fact that the alley had become a source of fascination to my children? The *big kids* hung out in alleys. My children were encouraged to stay in our yard. *You can have the whole neighborhood over, just stay in the yard.* How tempting the alley was. That was where the ice cream truck hovered and played *Turkey in the Straw*, like a pied piper.

"Please mommy, please mommy?" And that was when my kids were most polite. But that meant herds of kids scrambling to the ice cream man, waving their coins, and pushing others out of the way, while my kids were still begging. Most times, we were well supplied with ice cream by my Uncle Ernie DiNenna who owned the Tutti Frutti Ice Cream Distribution Company. He also had a few trucks, but his drivers packed a pistol as well as Nutty Buddys and Vanilla Cups. At that time, Baltimore City was in the lead for the prestigious title of *Murder Capital of The Nation.* I believe then we were in first place. Even though our freezer in the basement was full of ice cream, there was that truck in the alley and it was a legitimate chance to step out into it. This scenario played each day all summer long. Only a few times I can remember scraping my quarters together and watching by the gate as they patiently waited their turn to order, standing behind the wild, spindly arms of kids who rudely yelled, "Me first." I have to admit, it was a proud alley moment.

In the tradition of Academy Heights alleys, black men in white tank undershirts and straw hats sauntered alongside the clip clopping of old mangy workhorses who pulled dilapidated wooden wagons full of luscious red strawberries and heavy dark green watermelons. The men cupped their hands and their mellow reggae voices danced in the humid July air which Baltimore is famous for. Sometimes a baritone would sing *strawww bare eeess,* right along with the symphony of tree frogs and locusts. Those wagon wheels rolled down those cracked and patched alleys once a week. Crevices, craters, bumps, dips, rises. Whatever could go wrong with cement, was wrong with the alleys.

Do you know who were my alley buddies? *The trash men*, as we called them back then. During those years in the 1980's, I was either pregnant with a huge belly because all of my weight went there, or I was cuddling my little baby in my arms while watching the other children play in the yard. Those young, strong black men were most kind to me. If I should forget to push and pull those heavy cans, that might as well have been full of bricks, out to the alley, one of the men would stop me from running to the gate, with the a smooth, jazzy voice like the coolness of a saxophone. When it snowed, all I had to do was open the kitchen door. It was understood. Danny gave them beer for Christmas.

Alyssa became a victim of the alley's grizzly teeth. My red Caravan minivan was in the shop. We had to walk to Westowne Elementary that one October morning. I put Kelley into the baby stroller, all nestled with blankets, and I specifically told Anna to hold Alyssa's hand. This is the same little one who could wriggle out of a straight jacket, remember? Timmy forgot his coat so I raced back to the house to get it while the kids were still in the yard, gate shut. Michelle was now in Catonsville Middle School and already there by way of bus. How I wished we were in the right zone for bussing to Westowne. Now the gate is swung open and we have to walk briskly or they will be late. Of course, I believed I was doing the best I could so the word, *tardy*, had absolutely no meaning to me. I did not care how high the number soared on their report cards. If my children made it to school, I was pleased. My motto was: *Better late than never.* And I held onto it regardless of phone calls, letters, and rude comments made by the office. I knew for them, it was all about their school record and how they looked to the Baltimore County Board of Education. To me, it was all about the alarm clock, the one bathroom and eight of us brushing our teeth. I even wiped my baby's teeth clean when there were any. It was all about finding matching socks and shoes, shoving those papers and pencils inside their bookbags, making sure one or two of them had their notes for the teacher. There were always notes: *Please excuse Timmy for not doing his homework. He was ill . . . . Please excuse Anna for not completing her assignment. I made her go to bed. It was late. Please give her one more day . . . . Please give Danielle her medicine . . . and excuse her for not completing her homework. I will call you today. She is conscientious but frustrated . . . . No, I do not give permission for my child to attend the field trip . . . .* My hand ached. The first week of each school year I had to fill out five emergency cards for each child. That's 30 of them, all due the next day or else points were taken from their grade. Could they do that legally? A brilliant way to get kids to nag the hell out of their parents to complete those cards *NOW*. By the time high school invaded my household, writing late notes was a normal part of my morning routine, and I was as prepared as a Girl Scout. Pads of paper and pens were on top of the microwave for easy access. The kids all knew my motto and they fully lived up to it. Few people know what it is to get up and get going on time when there are so many things against you from the start. Like, *where are my car keys? What do you mean you cannot go to school ever again? Your hair looks fine . . .*

Just put it into a side pony tail . . . Yes, I'll do it as soon as I diaper the baby. What do you mean you don't want the crust on your bread? What do you mean you don't like soda? I can't afford those juice pouches. The soda is 10 cents a can. Trade with someone at school . . . . Okay, does anyone know where I just now put those car keys? You can't go to school like that. Change now. Oh my God, I need gas!

Comments were actually made by my own sister who lived within the bus zone, though she was only a block away, that I was speeding around the circle in front of the school building. Just because I halted my big red minivan to a jolting stop did not mean I was not respecting where I was. Okay, my brakes made a little bit of a screeching noise, I must admit, but speeding? Not I! Do you believe the office *still* did not abide by my motto? I was proud that my girls looked adorable and my son precious as they ran to the front door, arms flailing.

But on that one fall morning, we walked to school by way of the alley because it was the shortest route which proved to be the longest. The school had nothing but sympathy and understanding for us, smiling at us so sweetly. You see, it takes actual blood for people who work in a school office to feel any human kindness toward you at all. Anna had let go of Alyssa's hand because according to Anna, *she did not want me to hold it!* Down she fell flat into a mess of stones all jagged and glistening in the deep crevices of our delightful alley. Her face and coat were smeared with blood and tears. She was two years old and had a set of lungs on her like an Italian opera singer. *Oh Gesu Cristo, aiutarmi!* Oh God help me!

I stopped the bleeding from her mouth with pressure that was born out of my anger at Anna and my urgency to help my little daughter. Cold water on the coat and we headed out again on foot to go to school. Anna strolled baby Kelley and I held Alyssa in my arms as we trudged up hill on Northdale Road to get to the road that led to school. The ladies in the office finally saw what a struggle it was to get my children to school on time, but, they had to notice, I always got them there. I was true to my motto, *better late than never*, and anyway, on the average it was just 10 minutes late.

Of course, that morning, not only The Pledge Of Allegiance and Morning Announcements were over, but so was Reading. Alyssa's two front baby teeth were as jagged as those rocks. I had to take her to a pediatric dentist who was female and Alyssa liked her, especially since she first gave her laughing gas and lastly gave her a balloon and stickers. She felt like she had just come home from the circus. Needless to say, so did I.

Finally, I decided it was time to change up the scenery. So instead of being penned up in our tiny backyard jam packed with playhouse, swing set, sandbox, and a small cement pad Dan had poured for the pool and roller skating, we headed out to the playground. When we wanted a change from the mud holes at Christian Temple, we drove to the mud holes at the Rolling Road playground. My kids did what kids do best: run in the fields and slide down the slides. That's probably why they have all grown so tall. They passed my own 5 foot 3 a long time ago. My son is 6 foot 1, and with just a few inches heels, my girls are nearing 6 foot. Danielle is already there in flats. Danny and I would take them to Hillcrest Elementary to roller skate on the basketball courts on Saturdays. Playgrounds and library visits were the highlights of our family outings, until we bought a tent, but you already know how that went.

When did I ever feel relaxed about the alleys? Well never really. There was always a speeding car that just swooshed by us, nearly clipping the aluminum fence or scraping a parked car. Parking was a premium in row house living, so we did use the alley for one of our two vehicles. For Danny's work car of course. Later, he had a work truck, which makes more sense for a carpenter.

When it snowed and no school and Danny came home smiling like the sunshine on a cloudless day, as usual happy to see his family, he would pull the kids on a sled down the sleek alley, white with virgin snow. If they were too young, he would put them inside a cardboard carton and push them up and down the snow banks in our tiny, priceless yard, as well as the front slope. We could see their snowman waving at us from the front window. It was as fun as traipsing up and down the frozen ground searching for the perfect Christmas tree at the tree farm. We pulled the youngest on a sled who looked like a little snow baby, stuffed into a snowsuit with a furry hood. We sat in our car/van sipping steamy hot chocolate from stainless steel thermoses and eating Little Debbie snacks. We each had years of Little Debbies in our tummies because at that price I bought boxes and boxes. Of course we had Danny stomping all over the farm with his size thirteen construction boots and his bow saw to this tree and that, all of us believing we had found the right tree. *Hey Dad, over here! No Dad, over there!*

Danny got tired of mapping out the farm with his huge feet and his little bow saw. As usual, he would suddenly stop and cut the random tree right in front of him. *This is as good as any.* He always regretted making the first cut on multiple trees because we kept changing our minds.

If we go back to the alley one more time, I will tell you that the alley was a thoroughfare for any traveler. You never knew who or what would be passing by our back gate. A rat? A teenager up to no good? A raccoon? A fox? A stray cat or dog? How about a man who crouched down in the alley behind our parked car and then arose with a broken glass bottle in his right hand? It was midnight and I just happened to check on the children one more time and I saw him. I dared not put on a light, but I felt that he knew I was staring at him out the bedroom window. It looked like he boldly stared right back. We were deadlocked. I calmly went to my bedroom, did not wake up Danny, and dialed 911. Danny did wake up and we watched as the police car zoomed down the alley, high beams and siren and all. I was hoping the police would have been discreet and nabbed him, handcuffing him and pushing his head into the back seat for questioning. At least, that's what I always saw on TV police dramas. No chance of that. They just scared him off, and by doing so, left me feeling scared. That happened just two weeks after we had moved into the house. And that was the beginning of my loveless affair with the alley.

Funny thing, the more babies I had, the older the other children were looking. It is no wonder then, by the time Kelley was born there were raucous games of kickball in the alley. Michelle, Anna, and Danielle were emancipated and were running after the ball up and down the alley with their friends. It was a *coming of age*.

Chapter Eleven

WHO CAN I TALK TO OTHER THAN MOM?

For me, it was my Aunt Dottie who was only 16 years older than I. My mother never defended me. She always told me what I should have done and therefore, it is my own fault. My children accuse me of the *should have*'s and I must admit I do spew those hateful words into the air from time to time. But every mother will say that we say this to our children so they do not repeat those same mistakes in the future. Unfortunately, even with the best of intentions, that little phrase, *what you should have done*, is always interpreted as, *Mom thinks I am stupid*. Why is it that when we become mothers, we sometimes forget what we did not like about our own mothers, and we *become* our mothers in that memorable moment? It is something we mothers and mothers-to-be pass on from generation to generation. All that the *you should have* does, is confirm in the child's mind that mom just doesn't get it. So whenever I felt lonely and depressed and ugly, I would make my funeral march down the street and knock on my aunt's door. The good thing about her was that she could be impartial. She was not Italian, in fact she was of Swiss roots. She always had mountains of diapers to fold, numerous telephone calls to answer, toys to pick up, ashtrays to empty, a landslide of dishes in the sink, and me. She would give me a tissue and then sit me down and then give me her undivided attention. Dottie did this on the telephone with her sister and her cousin-in-law and whoever needed to talk. No *you should have's.* She would simply take your deflated self, restate your feelings, and then pump you up with all the good things about you, and how she was positive things were going to change for the better. She was my counselor throughout my teenage years because she was willing ;I was drawn to her kindness. My mother loved me dearly, but her response was always, *Get over yourself, Snap out of it,* as if I could chase all of those dark feelings away with the snap of a finger. Dottie had bought new clothes she was anxious to wear that summer. Dresses were hanging in her bedroom closet with price tags dangling from them. She had hung a photograph over the fireplace mantle of her new house she and Sal had just bought. She had one teen and three young children and a husband who owned two barber shops and who was the bass player in his very own jazz band. When Sal would come home at ten or eleven at night, Dottie would fry him a steak. Every time those two would go away together, Dottie would come home pregnant, or so it seemed to me. That one summer was hot and dry and Dottie was in her bed every afternoon with a pounding headache. I used to take the children up to my house so that the colorless sounds of silence could linger in hers. I was about 20 and I never missed a day where I did not wear hope like fine jewelry. I walked to her house with prayers in my heart but when I approached her bed, fear lunged at me and all my words of *you are going to get through this somehow* fell to the ground with a sickening thud. The last time I saw Dottie was in her hospital room. She accused me of flirting with her husband, Sal, my mother's brother. I felt like she had become a foreigner, someone whose language made no sense to me, someone I could no longer talk to. She told me to come closer while she held a cup of water. Sal told me not to get near her unless I wanted to get wet. None of this made any sense. Where did my friend go? Sal said it was time to go and the cup was on the tray, so I came close and grabbed her hand. She squeezed it and for a brief moment I had the affection of one who knew me well. Then she raised one hand upward and said," I guess I am going up there and I'll find out how great it is." I said, "No. You're not going anywhere."

I'll never forget that knowing expression and that peace upon her face. "Yes, I am." My father had that same knowledge when he looked at my mother and said, "Ann, I can't do this anymore." He was at peace because he had come to an agreement with death, that it was time. So Dottie passed on to that place worlds away from all the pain and grief on Earth. Any joy we have in this world is multiplied eternally to an unfathomable amount in heaven, I am sure. I know this just by the peace that I saw on Dottie's face, on my Uncle Ernie's face, and on my dad's face.

People come into our lives for a reason and for a season, as we come into theirs. We change and grow and learn to give. Mothers give even when their strength is gone, as fathers also give. It is then in the squeeze of her hand or that soft look in her eyes or in a whisper. And we do not fully realize this until we see her fragility yet feel her quiet strength. So it is and so it will be. Dottie died of a sudden brain tumor at the age of 37. Her youngest child was three. I had worn the beads of hope around my neck that summer, working and living in Ocean City, making a plan to work non-stop and save money for college so I would not have to work fall semester and I could give more time to Dottie, helping her through recovery. I randomly visited Palsie and Aunt Theresa that one morning, who were staying at the Beach Plaza. We had breakfast together. I was wearing the white blouse and black skirt uniform for Pappy's Restaurant. Uncle Frank called from home and talked with Aunt Theresa. She told us we had to go right home, that Dottie's operation was *that* day. I rode a bicycle down Coastal Highway and repeated those words to my boss like I was reading a script. *She has a brain tumor. I have to go.*

My aunt drove us home and right when we stepped inside Palsie's house, it hit me.

Perfect aim to the heart. Sarafina was telling Palsie that Dottie had died and telling me to run next door and get my mother, since Palsie was wailing and quaking. I ran next door to my house, not even remembering going up the stairs and entering my bedroom, and slammed the door shut. It sounded just like the ending of one's life. Nobody had told me. Nobody had considered me. I had just lost my soul mate who understood me the most. My mother said she had not known how to contact me. She was right. I had not called home yet. But if I had known how grave Dottie's condition was, I would have never left her side. By my mother "protecting" me, she left me most unprotected. I had lost my best friend, in fact, my only friend. The beads of hope burst and scattered every which way on the bedroom floor. How could I possibly gather them and will I ever want to wear them again? After the funeral, I had a first taste of motherhood. That summer, Diane and I lived with our cousins, helping them through their grief and ours any way we could. But every pot and pan, toss pillow, the telephone, the ashtray, red nail polish, the Rembrandt hung over the fireplace, reminded me of Dottie ; and looking at my cousins' faces reminded me of how much she loved her children. Barefoot Dottie with a cigarette in her hand, a telephone in her ear, and waving her arm for me to come inside. Baby Michael climbing on her like a tree as she sits down, exhausted. Stopping her car and picking up every old lady walking with grocery bags in her hand. Dottie with her short straight dark hair, fair skin, little nose she called *pugged*, and long legs. Dottie with a baby at her hip. This is how I remember her. "Sit down. I'm listening."

So what do I say to a daughter who complains that I was not there for her when she was 11 and needed to shave her legs and pluck her eyebrows? I did not take her into the bathroom for a clinical on female grooming. In fact, I never instructed any of my girls on how to do it. It was not even an issue for me at the age of 11. I was not allowed to shave until I was 13, so in the tradition of my mother's thinking, I thought the same. *You are not even a teenager!* How did I know my daughter was teased at school because her eyebrows met in the middle? So my oldest daughter was taught by her friends and she in turn taught her younger sisters when they turned the ripe old age of 11. Remember, I was always pregnant, nursing, or battling potty training from 1980-1993. I did not want the teenage years to come any sooner than they should. Alyssa says I did not let her shave for 5th grade graduation. No surprise here. I had by this time compromised that she could shave before entering middle school in late August. She was my 5th born. Right after the graduation ceremony in June, Alyssa was in our bathroom with Michelle and she was being taught how to shave and how to pluck. She says I had given her permission to do it right *after*, which makes no sense to me. The way I remember it, I saw a beaming little girl with smooth legs bouncing down the stairs and what could I say? It had begun, and once it starts, there's no turning back. Just like motherhood.

Mothers love their children fiercely. They are always wearing a full set of armor, ready to defend them to the death. I remember Michelle asking us if she could go to a dance with Abby on Easter night. Abby was a good friend of Michelle's. I knew her mother. The kids and I had been cast in a commercial for the Hilton Hotel and also been photographed for a brochure at her request. The girls had sleep overs together. I trusted Abby's mom. But that night, my brother Anthony enlightened me that where she had gone was an Under21 Club. Michelle was 12. I called the club and the woman who answered said, "I won't let *my* daughter come here." That's all I needed to hear. Danny and I drove to Towson in a flash. At the door, the bouncer told us that it is wall to wall packed with people and that if we wanted our daughter, then we have to go get her, ourselves. We swam through, literally holding our arms out so that people would move aside. Michelle looked over and there we were. Dan said only two words:

Let's go. To this day, Michelle says she will never forget the humiliation. I remember her glaring at us, and how many boys there looked 21. I did not want her to grow up that fast. Nope. Some things your children will never understand until they become parents, themselves.

So who did my children confide in when they became teenagers? Besides their all-important friends, to each other. We had lost our connection for a while, but I knew it would turn back on when high school years were lived and lost. We all need someone to talk to and who knows you better than the one who wore that armor for you all those years?

Chapter Twelve

THE TRESTLE TABLE

Ask any mother and she will tell you that the most important part of the day is dinner time. That is when the family talks to each other face to face and shares their day.

But little by little, family members start to disappear at that hour because of jobs or sports or invitations. Michelle got her first job at the age of 15 and it was at McDonald's. Time to keep my car keys nearby and time to buy a microwave. On Sundays, she had to be there before 5 a.m. Need a more annoying alarm clock.

Gregg, our friend who, along with his wife Karen, had introduced Dan and I, also introduced us to the trestle table. He sold us one six feet long in dark pine with two benches. In our Lochearn cottage, the table swallowed up the tiny dining room space. There were tiny Michelle and Anna on the bench and Dan and I at each end, all spread out like the rich people do. Within the next 6 years, we filled those benches. In our Academy Heights rowhouse, we had all six of our children side by side on benches with Danny and I on the ends in oversized wooden colonial chairs. Our quiver was full. Our table was hectic and life was good.

During my high school years, my best friend was Suzanne, a skinny girl with straight brown hair. She lived in a sprawling cottage home in Catonsville that had two staircases on the main floor and then two upper floors of just bedrooms. She is one of fourteen children. Her mother was a small little thing who had a huge kitchen table with benches, of course. On a bench, you can always slide over and squeeze another one in. Suzanne's mom always looked so small sitting at that table and I marveled how she had birthed all of those children. She always wore a bun in her light brown hair and had on a house dress like that of a country woman, kind of like Auntie Em in *The Wizard of Oz* but younger and prettier. Because the dining room table is always reserved for actual dining, only her kitchen table was used. They ate in two shifts. I'll never understand that. So when my mind drifted away from all of the weekly, wild parties at her house, Suzanne and I going from room to room picking out those boys we wanted to kiss and what kind of drink we would get sick on this Saturday night, there were so many choices, I started to think about that table and how everyone gathers there. Even though I had a crush on her older brother,Billy, and our lips had met, he was 24 and I was barely 17 so I was not thinking about having babies any time soon. Still, when I thought about my own family some day, I had decided I would buy a big table. It would give me a strong sense of belonging and knowing who I am, a mother with a large table and no room to spare. This was my mission in life. I just needed to find a soul mate with the same.

Our trestle table was our everything table. We ate every supper on it. We celebrated every birthday at it. When we visited the library and came home with our 60 books, we turned it into a book perusing center where we all got familiar with all that we had checked out. During the school year, it became the homework table after dinner. Whenever there was a school project, it was covered with materials and tools. And it was my accounting table where I paid my bills and kept my ledger of credit and debit.

What I love about our table is that it has an easy going personality. Pine welcomes nicks and markings because it just gives it more character. It can be wiped down every day without worry of stripping the finish. No polishing required. It is as imperfect as we are and that is what makes it perfect. To this day, the trestle table is the focal point of my dining room even though our children are grown. Eating there is backpacking through memories, like the time Timmy left the bench after dinner with the tablecloth somehow caught under his arm, dragging with him the plates, bowls and platters with left over food that cascaded to the wooden floor below. His little boy body kept right on moving to another room, unshaken by the catastrophe. He never looked back. Dan and I were frozen, just staring at the mess. We did not know if we were more stunned by the recent events or by Tim's nonchalant attitude. He was six. Other things on his mind like his little cars. Oh, and that huge dinner party we gave while I was still nursing Alyssa, number 5. I had made six large pans of lasagna the Saturday before which took me all day. I hired Mindy and Amy from across the alley to help serve and to do all the dishes. Excellent job and very sweet girls. You would think I had it all covered! The trestle table was packed. We set up card tables throughout the living room. Tablecloths, wine glasses, fancy napkins, candles . . . . Besides nursing the baby and keeping my children in their beds, and directing Amy and Mindy, and keeping the kitchen as organized as I could, Danny and I were helping to serve the lasagna and pour the wine, and making sure the Italian music kept on playing. What I had anticipated to be an enjoyable evening for all, had excluded Dan and I. After we finally had sat down and eaten and the plates were all cleared, our guests were putting on their coats to go home because they had church in the morning and because they had to drive their babysitters home. I had even made party favors for the women, a gingham circle of material drawn tight by a wooden hoop with a wooden carved animal figure glued in the center, to hang on a closet door or elsewhere, since all of us were crazy for country at that time. There were 17 couples at our rowhouse that Valentine's night. I swore I would never do that again, at least never with people who thought 10 o'clock on a Saturday night was late. Danny and I did not even get to relax and talk with our guests. We were nothing but restaurant managers, servers, and maitre d's.

In the dining room window we had a large old fan, sounding like the propeller of an airplane. In the adjoining living room, we had a window air conditioner, so it was never quiet and peaceful, but who wants that anyway? Dinner was full of sounds: clinking and clanking and gabbing and laughing and complaining and scolding and crying and laughing.

By the time we moved the trestle table to our new home in Carroll County, it had grown fuzzy with white flannel that had permanently stuck to the surface because of the humidity within the walls of our house on Regent Park Road. Remember, our rowhouse was a middle and it cooked us in the summer. I should have never resorted to a vinyl tablecloth. We found someone to refinish it, The Country Stripper, (my girls thought it was the name of my new job, since I had it hanging on the refrigerator and they knew I was job hunting). So the trestle table was given new life and a place of honor in our new home. It was placed in the dining room, then in the kitchen, and then back into the dining room, but has never left the front door and never will if up to me. Its simple, laid back style suits us. In a way, it defines us, the closeness we've shared over the years, and the promise that in the years ahead we will remain so, no matter what.

CHAPTER THIRTEEN

WESTOWNE

The elementary school for Michelle, Anna, Danielle, Timmy and Alyssa was Westowne, the school we kids always thought was so easy compared to our catholic school, St. Agnes. We used to envy the public school kids whose arms were free coming home each day while ours were heavy laden with schoolbooks. How come they never got homework? Now my kids were going there but times had changed. I soon grew weary of all the homework I had to do, oops, I mean *help with*. Sometimes it was just less painful to choose the vocabulary for them when writing paragraphs. I'd look at it as *modeling* in hopes that next time they could be more selective with language and more careful with grammar. When the children transferred to Carroll County Public Schools, Michelle was finishing middle school, Anna was beginning, Danielle was in the 4th, Timmy 2nd, and Alyssa, kindergarten. So Alyssa only had a brief school career with Westowne. Kelley did not know it at all.

What bothered me was the news, one report after another of someone with evil in his heart, easily entering an elementary school and shooting children. Even the Amish in Lancaster was not exempt. St. Agnes School had a locked door and a buzzer. Westowne had nothing and it was only a few blocks away from there. If the Catholic Church felt it necessary, why didn't the public school? It also played on my mind that on the first day of school that year, a man in a parked car had unzipped his pants and was exhibiting himself to every child who stepped down from the bus. Teachers only locked the back doors which were propped open whenever the kids had recess or physical education. The front door remained unlocked for anyone to enter,whether you worked at the tile company next door, or lived in the apartments across the street, or escaped from Spring Grove Mental Hospital just a few miles down the road, or drove up from Baltimore City on a joy ride, the city line being only a few blocks away. The invisible sign read: ALL Are Welcome No Matter Your State Of Mind. Here I am home behind locked doors and my children who are more precious to me than my very own life, are unprotected for those 6 hours every day. I had to do something.

Surprised that no other parent even thought about it, I began to solicit interest among the mothers I did know. I asked the principal for her support, someone new to the area but she listened all the same. I said, *Just because nothing significant has happened thus far does not mean we do not have cause for concern.* She agreed but warned that if approved by The Board, our request would be at the bottom of the list as it read that day. Not a priority. That could mean two to three years. Amazing. I requested time at the next PTA which she granted me. After I spoke about our troubled times and how precious our children are, one parent said that because he leaves his car unlocked and nothing ever happens, he sees no reason for action to be taken. I asked him if his children were worth more than, say, his car? Not one parent was in agreement with me; however, I had interested the principal who was a hefty, large woman with a booming heavy voice and she was slowly becoming well liked. by the parents in Catonsville.

After having written 17 letters to senators, county executives, the mayor, and principals from public schools in the area, I had received no satisfaction until I saw the evening news one night and heard the interview of a Fairfax County Public School principal. He had instituted the buddy system with his elementary school children, and their front door was now locked with a buzzer and camera, and monitor inside the front office. Exactly what I wanted. I wrote to him immediately. He quickly responded by letter, explaining in detail what he had initiated and why. I made a copy and gave it to our principal who was on the verge of petitioning The Board. Her mind was now made up. We were added to the waiting list within two weeks, although Westowne did not make it to the top of the list until two years later. By that time, my kids had transferred out to Carroll County where to this day, the front doors are open. Anything can happen anywhere, but our little town of Eldersburg is relatively safe and that is why we moved here. At one Westowne PTA, my sister had helped me distribute the letter I had written to the parents, informing them of what I was trying to do and why. Nothing came of it. Thanks to the Fairfax County principal and ours, Westowne Elementary children now have a safer building in which to learn. There is a locked front door with a buzzer and a security camera, and a monitor in the front office. What can just one mother do? Change the world.

A few years after we moved away, the news reported of an elementary school child bringing a gun to school and fatally shooting another child. This story started a wave of others, perhaps the most tragic being Columbine High School in Colorado. No child in school is safe anymore, a sad statement on our society and the parents who are afraid to discipline their own children for fear that Social Services might become involved for no good reason. Teachers are afraid to discipline their students because students have rights and teachers are stripped of all authority. Schools still refuse to install metal detectors at their entrance doors. They say it will slow down their morning schedules. They just don't have the time. How much time does it take for a bullet to enter the flesh after the gun is shot? How much time does it take for a vibrant life to be snuffed out? While the smoke is still encircling the gun like a halo, criminals have rights. A middle school boy walked right through the front door of Oklahoma Road Middle, a Carroll County Public School my children attended. He walked into the lavatory during first period and shot a gun he had concealed. It ricocheted off of the wall and missed him. Fortunately, no other child was in there. The librarian, all 5 feet of her, ran in there and escorted him to the office. That was in 2004 and Kelley was in the 8th grade there. I was in the school library. I heard the shot. Do you think that Carroll County addressed that issue? Not at all. The boy was sent to alternative education for the rest of the year but allowed to start high school at Liberty the following fall. Earlier, there had been an issue in 2001 at Liberty High where my children attended and I taught English. My daughter Danielle was told by a boy whose sister had heard that a certain troubled boy at Liberty who was "picked on", was going to make a bomb through the internet and he made a list of those students he hated. A teacher had it. I immediately told the principal and it fell on deaf ears. Because I told other teachers, he was forced to suspend him. What? So he can have more time to make bombs? Needless to say, I was then not well liked by that principal who from then on gave me unfavorable evaluations. I was told to resign from Carroll County Schools. Not to mention, I had taught Bible Literature at Westminster High the year before and was railroaded out of there because I had taught Sodom and Gomorrah and the parents of one girl were two

Lesbians. The parents threatened to sue the county, accusing me of preaching. I was not. What is written is written. The day that 9 week course ended, I was told by the principal that I was being transferred. At Liberty High, my next school, I taught 5 classes of American Literature without being given my own room. I was given 5 of them. Every day I lugged two heavy tote bags up and down crowded halls, rushing to get to class in time to get organized in each new environment. When I taught *The Adventures of Huckleberry Finn*, an American classic, I was reprimanded by the principal and two assistant principals because I had read parts of it out loud word for word to my students, who were having trouble with the dialect. I was told by a black mother that I was to have the students read it silently. She was at conference with me and accused me of being racist. I was told by the principal to change the *N* word to "slave." I said, "So, now you are changing history?" My students had been instructed about America in the 1850's. There was no excuse for the trouble a single student out of 150 caused. Needless to say, I was denied tenure . . . So much for staying up until after 2 a.m.,correcting 150 essays, as I did more often than not. So much for my well earned career as an English teacher. Here I am with 27 credits beyond my BA. There are other counties. True. But the State of Maryland has denied me certification, punishing me for staying home all those years to raise my family. No day care center for my children! I did not have children to just hand them over to just anybody. Maryland says that by now, I should have my Master's or Master's Equivalency. I am nine graduate credits shy, but I cannot independently fund its completion. So here I am, writing.

The truth is, I tried to pursue my career and during that time, I took care of my family of 8 as well as my 150 students.

I put my heart into it. I have no regrets. If I had to do it over again, I would still have put my career on hold and stayed with my children 24-7. It is what I chose to do just by giving birth. When Kelley was one, I returned to the classroom, teaching high school at night. Six years later, I substitute taught long term at Liberty High. When I signed a contract for Carroll County, I was told to earn 24 credits in two teaching years. I earned 15. So I guess I would not have been hired back at any rate. But I cannot help but think that if they had supported my right to teach literature as it is written, then they would have given me more time in which to complete my certification.

What is a career anyway, in the end? If we compromise our integrity and deny the truth, what is our life worth? Our character and our beliefs are all that matters in the end, that and how much we have loved each other. Getting back to Westowne, our first school experience, there was one situation that evolved into a real crisis. New renters had moved in next door to us. That meant we heard them pounding up and down their steps as if they were ours. One night about two o'clock, my heart almost stopped as I stood there in the hallway, frozen, thinking someone was thumping up *my* stairs in the dark. Amanda, the chubby girl next door, "befriended" our skinny little daughter, Michelle. Amanda and her brother, Tim, loved to hang out at our house. Now this is the house where the parents dressed in black and left the house at midnight, where the shades were always drawn, and the answering machine was recording messages at the speed of lightening. It did not take long before Amanda started lying, accusing Michelle of labeling her drawing of Amanda as *the fat one*. We all knew Amanda had labeled it herself Then things started getting more bizarre. She would go to Bible School on Wednesday nights with my children, carrying her Bible in hand and with her Arkansas accent, say that she loves God's word. As soon as I dropped them off, she would ditch the Bible and the school and go hiding in the bathroom and roaming the halls, dragging Michelle with her. Pretty soon, she was saying she did not want to go to Bible School anymore, being that the last time she went, they were caught and made to actually attend the class. After that, things got weirder.

How devious she was for a fifth grader. One by one, Amanda started to steal Michelle's friends from her by telling them lies. When I saw the girl up the street approaching Amanda's house for a sleep-over, I stopped her and told her what Amanda's plan was, to turn everyone against Michelle and to do it by lying. This was the only girl in Michelle's class who was *still* speaking to her. The mother, Tess, ran out to me, her nightgown flowing, staring at me with her dead eyes, her face in my face, and sneered," You are a pitiful person." She grabbed that little girl and whisked her away into her house and slammed the door. On Monday, as soon as school hours resumed, I was calling the guidance counselor. She spoke separately with both Amanda and Michelle. She told me that she knew Amanda was lying. Things got worse.

No one in Michelle's class spoke to her. When Michelle tried to speak to anyone, she or he would turn her or his back to my daughter. Meanwhile, every day I am speaking with the guidance counselor, Debra, who told me that clearly we are dealing with an evil situation. Debra became my prayer partner as we joined forces against this slanderous, malicious spirit that resided in my neighbors next door. One morning, Michelle, dressed in her skirt and blouse, her waist length hair brushed, her shoes on, sat on her bed, the top bunk, and said matter of fact *that she was not going to school anymore.* I immediately called Debra who said that now this is a matter for the administration. The assistant principal told the class to put their heads down and raise a hand if they have ever had a fight with Michelle or if they have ever heard Michelle say anything mean to them, or to another about them. Only Amanda raised her hand. All other hands were down. He told the class to look up at him. Then he said that the *blackballing* stops here and now. It will not be tolerated and parents will be called. Then he called me and told me to bring in Michelle. I was proud of my daughter. She went to school that day, bravely putting her hurt feelings aside. Danny had tried to speak to Tess, but she just cussed him out. He left her house quickly before he said something he would later regret. Tess called the school and said she was suing them. The school stood their ground and firmly said that this was a neighborhood matter, and not a school issue, so she had no grounds. Tess dropped the threat. She had called the police on me a week before, accusing me of restraining that little girl who was visiting her daughter, you know, the last one she needed to poison against Michelle. The officer visited me, spoke with me, then went next door and spoke with her. He came back to me and told me, "Have nothing to do with *that woman.*

Not even a wave of the hand. Remember, nothing. All you can do is pray."

That confirmed it. We were dealing with *evil.* It is a real entity. Can be living right next door. That opened my eyes. My favorite Scripture from then on? "No weapon that is formed against me, or my family, shall prosper; and every tongue that rises against us in judgment, You shall condemn. This is my heritage and my family's. We are servants of the Lord. Our righteousness is of the Lord." (Isaiah 54:17)

Chapter Fourteen

HEAT WAVE

Baltimore summers are hot and humid, sticky and stifling, sauna like, greenhouse like and tomatoes and peppers grow plump in sunny bright reds and greens. But people sweat and drip and wilt. My neighbor Ann, across the alley, invited us all to sleep at her house that evening. Dan felt awkward and said he would stay behind. I sent all six children over and they spent the night curled up in blankets. I couldn't leave Dan to sweat all alone so, being the good wife that I am, I vowed to sweat with him, side by side. Being a woman, I thought it a good opportunity to lose weight. It was unusually warm. The air was so still that you could not hear a single cricket or a the slightest chirp of a bird. Nothing was moving. Not even a whisper of a breeze. The stars were dim and the moon was fuzzy. The only thing that was clear was that the ceiling fan was working hard to circulate the heavy woolen blankets of air throughout our bedroom. I wanted to unzip my skin and step out. I did not want even the side of Dan's leg to touch me as we lay side by side with eyes closed trying to sleep. I had an idea, as one would trapped in the merciless grip of the desert. We need a waterfall. Just like in the desert, it proved to be a mirage. We turned the lever in the shower down as low as it could go and stepped into a rejuvenating cascade of icy, refreshing water, drenching every pore in our skin with new life. Upon leaving the bathroom, we were attacked in the hallway by the grizzly heat and soon dried up. Danny was used to working outside in the construction field, in mammoth ditches and on rooftops, bandanna on his head like a pirate, gulping water every 15 minutes,wiping his brow . . . but after doing that all day long, this was like a cruel punishment. We lay in bed moist from the shower and within a few minutes, we are baking on the hot coals of night again. Every half hour, we were groping for the shower. Just like a mirage, the coolness was not real. It quickly melted. Danny had an idea. Soak wash cloths with cold water and wrap them around our feet. We did it. We did it again. And again. And so it went on throughout the night. In those days there was no Reality TV. If there were, maybe I could have remembered an episode of Survivor. There was no PC so I could not Google :*How can I survive a heat wave without air conditioning?* In the morning I telephoned my dad to tell him about our night and the rags on our feet. He said, "Pack your bags and spend the weekend with us." Anthony got on the phone and said it was so cold in his bedroom last night that he had winter blankets and flannel pj's. Of course, he was just rubbing it in like he always did. For some reason, the *rags on our feet* was the funniest thing he had ever heard! We could not afford central air so we had fans. The AC window unit had been pushing out gusts of slightly cool air into the living room that were not strong enough to battle the fierce heat, so Dan said he was going to repair it. Being a bona fide procrastinator did not help. When he finally got around to it and was actually working on it, he accidentally kind of cut the Freon line. Sadly, he had to plop the air conditioner by the curb and just walk away.

Another kind of *heat,* the kind I appreciate, is the police. More than once, I made the call for them to put pressure on someone. I always called the State Troopers because Eldersburg is so small that we do not have our own police force. I called for Anna because a young man she knew kept filling up her voice mail with raw, crude comments. The officer found him in a parking lot hanging out with his friends. He took him aside and threatened that Anna was going to press charges so he never phoned her again. Another time was when Tim' s feet were bitten by a vicious dog, half Shepherd and half Rottweiler. He was invited inside the house of his "friend" and then he was attacked. The officer visited the unconcerned mother and visited the vet to make sure the killer dog had his shots. Tim did not press charges but the officer was willing to take it a step further if Tim had wanted to do so. I called the Humane Society and Animal Control, asking them to see to it the dog gets put down. Any child who was attacked by that animal would not stand a chance. Upon no provocation, the dog had attacked Tim and it took three people to finally get his teeth off of my son. It was two a.m. and I was speed driving Tim to the Emergency. Once there, I helped him into a wheelchair because his feet were so swollen he could not walk. After many questions and many bandages, I took him home. Next morning, I called the State Trooper who was immensely helpful. He talked to the owners and to their vet. The dog was up to date with shots. He made a trip to the vet to see the papers for himself. My neighbor Sam, a lawyer, investigated also and found they did not have homeowners insurance. No money for compensation. Both Tim and I lost time at work. Tim did not want to press a civil suit which he later regretted when he realized this kid was no friend of his.

Other times the Westminster Police had come to my house under somewhat graver circumstances having to do with deep depression and suspicion of marijuana. They were polite and genuinely concerned. I understand that the men with the badges are here to help us. I also understand that as a parent, I must recognize my kids' mess-ups as welcomed signals to me. They become the life preservers they hang onto inside the torrent ocean when we parents did not even know there was a storm, let alone our kids were caught in the crosscurrents. The police are here to help us get through it in any way they can. I know that young people see the police as "the heat", out to get them, but in the end, the truth is, they are out to *save them*. "All things work together for good to those who love God and are called according to His purpose." (Romans 8:28). All things.

Those nights a policeman would call and tell us to pick up our child from some unsupervised party, I was grateful. Tim and I trekked out to Howard County 2 a. m. to pick up Alyssa. Other parents who gathered there in front of the apartment complex were grumbling. I was grateful to put my daughter into the truck with us. I thanked the officer

That time Michelle did not show up for Lindsay's baby shower, a childhood friend, and I knew she had driven up from the Eastern Shore for it, I got the police involved. Dan and I were scavenging the phone book, looking for numbers of her friends. Like detectives, we narrowed our search down to a single house where Michelle was last seen at a party the night before. The father who answered the door was evasive and guarded. Michelle was not there, even though he said he thought she had spent the night. I told him I was going to call the police. The police said they would check out this man's story and that I did have cause for alarm. Two hours after the shower had started Michelle called me, knowing of our recent visit. She came home and we grabbed our presents and left for Catonsville. We did not speak about it but Michelle was fuming. I never apologized for tracking her down. One day she may do the same. A mother will travel to the ends of the earth for her children, knocking on a million doors until she sees her child's face.

Chapter Fifteen

SLEEP OVERS

They were always a big deal. *Who are the parents? Will they be home? What is their phone number? We will meet them when we drop you off, or we'll have a "phone conference."* "OH, MOM!" was always the response. After all, the parents could be perverts or alcoholics or bi-polar. Who knows? I realize that you don't know a person just by saying hello, but I always feel that if you see my face then you will feel accountable to me. I like to make myself known, like at the bank, at the school, at my child's place of employment, at a sleep over . . . . I always felt a lot more comfortable when the sleep over was at my house. *Why don't you invite your friend here?* Of course that defeats the purpose of a sleep over for *my* child. What usually happened was the other child loving to be a part of our large family and wanting to sleep over again and again. We had a lot of them. When we moved to the new house, Timmy wanted one. I didn't know boys liked that sort of thing. In the morning I knew why. Food was everywhere, stuck to walls and smeared on the floor of my brand new white kitchen.

Here I was sleeping peacefully upstairs, glad my son was in his own house, and the boys were engaged in a food fight! I swore never again, but when Tim was older, now in Middle School, I figured he was more mature and would not do anything a baby would do. I was right! An officer called me at 4:00 in the morning to tell me that he had picked up my son and his friend who were strolling down Route 26, two miles away, smoking cigars, which they had purchased at the 7-11 Store. *What?* Dan was just getting up for work so he volunteered to drive the friend home. So much for sleep overs when you have a trap door in the basement where your son's bedroom is.

When Michelle and Anna had sleep overs as little girls, Danielle would always be crying because she felt left out. Then again, Danielle would cry when it was her sister 's birthday and not hers. And then again, when it was *her* birthday, she swooped up all of her presents into her arms, refusing to share them or even let her sisters look at them. Or even her guests. They always had birthday parties with a lot of children, games, balloons, ice cream and cake. My husband could not understand this. Growing up, he never even had a birthday party. *"Awww, Danielle, that's not nice"*, he would say. Through the years, he must have said *that's not nice*, about a thousand times, to each of them Like when the girls took each others' clothes without asking, sometimes as pay backs . . . . like when they would slap each other or scream at each other or push each other or whatever else sisters do to each other because they love each other. Timmy would never raise a hand to his sisters. Danny taught him well. The one time Danny was most angry at me, he punched a hole right through the wall and then he apologized. To this day, we cannot remember why he was so upset. We just remember the hole and how much we love each other.

Chapter Sixteen

GRANDPARENTS

Every Sunday after church, we religiously visited our parents, the grandparents.

We ate breakfast at the Steinnagel's and dinner at the Aquila's. We brought diapers and the port-a-crib. Both grandmothers had high chairs at their houses. It was a long day of eating and talking and playing with the children. We brought their pajamas and before we left they were in them. Danny and I stayed out late with the children and they were used to it. My mom had the best dinners. Often she served crab cakes, bottom round roast beef, and turkey cutlets coated with Italian bread crumbs and Romano cheese and fried in olive oil. Always crusty bread, tossed salad, and three varieties of vegetables not including potatoes. Always a home made pound cake made of three sticks of butter and five eggs, or a creamy cheesecake, or an ice cream parfait. We all sat around the kitchen table that had two leaves in it and of course, a tablecloth, that Mom would just shake out when it was time for dessert. I cannot even remember when we stopped our Sunday tradition. I guess we stopped going to Danny's mom and step-dad's house when they stopped speaking to us because we changed our name to Cook, Danny's birth name. I suppose we stopped dining with my parents when the children had jobs and we had to drive them there, and it was getting too hard to do so from Mom and Dad's. We still visited but not necessarily for dinner, although there were still many more dinners to be had there, a lot of times with Diane and her family as well . . . At Christmas and Easter, all of us were gathered at the dining room table as well as the kitchen table, as well as the two card tables in the family room. We could see each other pretty much from each room.

At Christmas, it was Mom's biscotti, with lemon icing colored green and red with sprinkles on top. For Easter, it was Mom's biscotti with lemon icing colored pastel green and pink. For Danny, it was a personal can filled with Apricot Biscotti with a lemon glaze. For me, it was enough. I've had biscotti all of my life. It is our signature, fattening cookie.

No one can accuse us of not sharing our children with the grandparents. No one can accuse my mother of not giving her all to her grandchildren. It was all about sleep overs, going shopping, eating whatever they wanted, and staying up late playing cards and laughing with Nonna. Pop-Pop just paid the Visa bills. But he loved filling his house with the sound of little feet and little giggles.

This explains why Anna wanted to be stranded at Nonna and Pop-Pop's in a snowstorm, and why she begged to go there when she was in tears and upset with life, itself. She would pack her little suitcase and try to sneak out with my parents whenever they came for a visit. She was often unsuccessful. It was usually a Sunday night during the school year. Danielle must have thought that if it was all the rage with her older sisters, she must be missing out. So that explains her begging to spend the night with my parents, her very first sleep over. It is ten o'clock at night and little Danielle takes one look at her grandparents, all cozy on the sofa in their pajamas and she in hers, and she says," I'm not staying in a place like this." My father shoots up like a rocket and says, "Let's go." Within a half hour, we were answering the knock on our door. Danielle was about 6 years old and obviously, very attached to her home, which I say is just fine with me.

Timmy was in the middle of a household of girls. He was always laughing because what else could he do? For a while, he had a nervous tic and he would lick his lips until they were permanently outlined in red. Dr. Nuri, our dentist, was concerned and told him to put Chapstick on and don't even think about licking. Tim outgrew it and from then on, the only time his lips swelled was when we were at the ocean and he spent all afternoon catching waves on his Boggy Board. There was always Benedryl. When Tim was a teenager and working hard at Chili's and at school, he would just walk out of the house at times, saying, "There's too much PMS in this house! I let him go without telling me where he was going because all he would say was, *out.*

Kelley, being the youngest, was influenced by her sisters in what to wear and also, how to get into a club with a fake I.D. The 5 inch Jessica Simpson heels, the Sophora make-up, the oversized cocktail rings, the short flirty dresses, the skinny jeans, all part of *Cook Couture.* Tim can be seen in a Chili's tee and athletic pants, or gym shorts, tee shirt and running shoes. He is as health conscious as the girls are fashion conscious. I'm a bit of both. Danny is Danny. Clueless. I think he was born that way. But *someday over the rainbow where bluebirds fly and dreams do come true,* Danny and I want to be called Boopa and Grampa, the grandparents, the *still-young grandparents,* that is.

A Final Note

Being a mother is the most honorable profession of them all. A mother is the instrument through which Humanity harmonizes with Nature. Babies born and nurtured with love become adults who, in turn, give nurturing and love. A parent is given the most awesome of responsibilities, to watch over a life born in God's image, and to shape that life into something beautiful, purposeful, and worthy of the calling. Wisdom is calling. Do we hear her? The Lord is calling. Are we listening? Do we, as parents, take our role seriously? Do we realize that all eyes are on us and that we are being analyzed and criticized, maybe even judged, by our children, maybe even on a daily basis? It is what it is.

Each of my six children is different, from the color of their eyes, to the texture and color of their hair, to their stature, to the shape of their noses and to the size of their feet. They have green eyes, blue eyes, hazel eyes, and brown eyes. They have very curly hair and wavy hair and straight hair. They are blondes and brunettes. Danielle is almost 6 feet, and Kelley is 5 foot 4 like me. I have a son who resembles his father in coloring and stature, but feature to feature resembles the Brocato side of my family. In Michelle's, Anna's and Alyssa's faces, I see the union of our two families. In Danielle's and Toni Kelley's faces I see only my father, my grandmother Aquila, and me. We are products of our family tree and the genes and traits that shape us. Alyssa is as loquacious as Timmy is quiet. Michelle is confident and Anna unsure. Danielle has poise and grace. Kelley is straight forward and matter-of-fact.

As different as each one is, there is something that identifies us as *family.* There is a resemblance that resonates we belong to each other. Is it in our faces or the sound of our voices, or is it our mannerisms or the way we walk, or our choice of words? Is it in our quickness to defend like Alyssa, or is it in our quiet reflectiveness like Timothy? Is it in our fierce faithfulness to each other like Michelle, or our easily frustrated nature like Danielle? Is it in our quest to head out on our own with confidence, like Kelley? Is it in our wanting to know what is going on with each one of us, like Anna? Is it in the wanting for each one of us to be happy, like I do? Is it in the deep desire of the heart that we shall always be close, always be here for one another, like Danny hopes? I believe it is all of this that makes us the family we are. Timmy and Danny think before they speak. The girls and I? Not so sure. Who we are is *what* we are, that which runs through our veins. Different yet the same.

There is a purpose here. There is a plan. There is a reason God chose us to be a family at this point in time for all eternity. It is exciting, fearful, and awesome. It is tears of joy and tears of sorrow, and tears just for the sake of tears. It is suffering and it is healing. It is hoping and losing hope, and then finding it again. It is broken hearts made new. It is broken dreams repaired and visions resurrected. It is the life of family. As long as we believe that God loves us and that He gives us the grace to continue loving each other, no matter what, we can get through anything. Each one's life journey is his own, but we never have to walk alone. Each one is special. We must believe in ourselves and trust that the decisions we make are the right ones. We are family.

. . . "Lo, children are an heritage of the Lord, and the fruit of the womb is His reward."

(Psalm 127: 3)

In the beginning of this little book, I mentioned that *regrets* are like roadblocks and we must take detours to get back on track. Make no mistake, regrets need to be tamed or they will devour you. Do I regret that we spanked Danielle again and again, thinking she was willfully disobedient when all the time, it was because she could not hear out of her left ear? The doctor missed it, we missed it, and Danielle was too young and unsophisticated to be able to discriminate and tell us that she could not hear . . . Do I regret that I did not spend more time with Timmy when Danny was taking jobs out of town and working overtime like crazy? Timmy was missing his dad so much that he wrote him this really long letter pouring out his heart to him, begging him to spend more time with him. He wrote, "You are the most important person in my life. I want you home." He was only 8 . . . . Do I regret that I was not brave enough to send Anna and Danielle to Camp Hashawa in Carroll County when all of the other six graders went, and my reason was because we are newcomers? . . . Do I regret that I did not praise my children as much as I criticized them, thinking I was helping them? . . . . Do I regret that I did not have as many heart-to-heart talks with my teenagers as they probably needed? Do I regret that we slacked on disciplining Alyssa and Kelley because we were too tired to put forth that much effort? Do I regret not getting to know Alyssa's and Kelley's high school teachers and I stayed away from Liberty High just because I had a bad experience there? . . . Do I regret not giving Kelley more attention, spending so much time on my school work for jobs that never lasted very long, anyway?

Do I regret not trusting in Michelle's judgment when she went out with her teenage friends and working myself up to a panic? Do I regret putting a Biblical tone on each and every situation so that my children kept serious secrets and would not confide in me for fear of judgment? Do I regret sharing some information about my children with my sister and my mother because I trusted them to be supportive instead of judgmental? . . .

Do I regret not teaching my girls how to apply make up and style their hair when they were approaching high school? . . . As sure as I breathe, I do!

So what do I do with all of this stuff that I clearly still remember and think about? I erase all excuses. I admit I was wrong. To my children I am saying, *I am sorry from the deepest places of my heart.* To myself, I am saying, *I forgive me.* The Bible says that "Love covers a multitude of sins." (1 Peter 4:8) I am choosing to leave it all in the past and I am trusting in love. I am throwing into the wind all of the dust and the debris it leaves behind, letting it blow away into the sea. I am purposing to see the good in every situation, realizing that all of those hurtful, regretful, thoughtless moments of our lives are part of life's journey, and we must take a detour, making them our t*eachers* instead of our *tormentors*, so we can get back on the road to peace. What are regrets, anyway? Only reminders that we are human and flawed, and who are we kidding? Only God is perfect, anyway. We cannot go back and relive them and this time get it right. We all depend on mercy. In the end, all that matters is that we have loved each other with everything we've got deep down inside us, in the deepest parts of our soul and the unsearchable places in our heart.

To Michelle Rose, Anna Maria, Danielle Christine, Timothy Daniel, Alyssa Kathleen, and Toni Kelley Simona, I say that I love your strengths and your vulnerabilities, your capacity to love and to forgive, your resolve to get back up after taking a fall, your bravery to face each new challenge, even if it is a broken heart, your tears and your laughter, the sound of your voice, the feel of your hug, your faithfulness to each other, your willingness to right the wrong, and your passion for the truth no matter what it is. I love you as you are. No regrets.

ABOUT THE AUTHOR

Barbara Aquila graduated from University of Maryland with a BA in English Literature/Secondary Education. She taught American and British literature. She married Danny Cook, and together they have six children. They live in Eldersburg, Maryland where Barbara divides her time between her children, now grown, and the writing of her books.

CPSIA information can be obtained at www.ICGtesting.com
Printed in the USA
BVOW071847060612

291979BV00001B/12/P